More Praise for *Dot Boom*

"In the bumpy turbulence of our current market, David Weigelt and Jonathan Boehman skillfully navigate marketers through the thought processes of today's baby boomer. By introducing Developmental Relationship Marketing and Meaningful Online Engagement, they've created a systematic approach to obtaining 'landing rights' in the emotional mind of this powerful customer."

> — *Tom Mann, co-founder of Mature Market Experts and TR Mann Consulting and former senior vice president of advertising for* Erickson Retirement Communities

"David Weigelt and Jonathan Boehman understand the theory and, more importantly, the practice of engaging with older Web users. They have distilled their years of experience into the most readable book — *Dot Boom*. If you are working in digital media with a market of older online users, then this is essential reading."

> — *Dick Stroud, chief executive officer of 20plus30 and author of* The 50-Plus Market

"Bottom line, David Weigelt and Jonathan Boehman get it. In *Dot Boom*, they share their deep knowledge and practical experience on how to market to today's boomers online. In straightforward and clear language, they demystify and explain exactly what to do and how to do it. The examples they share bring it all to life. You won't go wrong reading this book."

> — *Matt Thornhill, founder and president of the Boomer Project and co-author of* Boomer Consumer

"The current credit crunch is making marketing departments look for improved ROI. *Dot Boom* is the solution to achieving this. The authors build a solid basis for the development of strategies for targeting mature consumers."

> — *Kevin Lavery, director of Millennium, managing director of Agency Group, and president of the International Mature Marketing Network*

"While the title implies online marketing, this book is a genuine heads-up for marketers in any space looking to target the ubiquitous baby boom generation. There's good reading, and great learning, here regardless of how well you think you already engage your target boomer consumers today."

> — *Kurt Medina, president of Medina Associates, co-author of* 77 Truths About Marketing to the 50+ Consumer, *and lead instructor for the Direct Marketing Association's "Mastering the 50+ Marketplace" seminars*

"The knowledge base of David Weigelt and Jonathan Boehman's research, the stats on the baby boomers as a target audience, and the concepts offered to identify, create, and establish relationships with these consumers are unmatched by any I've seen."

> — *Harby Tran, publisher of* Smart Company *magazine*

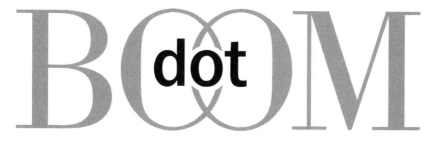

Marketing to Baby Boomers through
Meaningful Online Engagement

David   Jonathan
WEIGELT \\ BOEHMAN

With a foreword by David Wolfe
co-author of *Firms of Endearment*

Published by LINX
LINX, Corp. Box 613, Great Falls, VA 22066

Books are available for special promotions and premiums. For details, contact
Special Markets, LINX, Corp., Box 613, Great Falls, VA 22066,
or email specialmarkets@linxcorp.com.

THE LIBRARY OF CONGRESS HAS CATALOGED THE HARDBACK
EDITION AS FOLLOWS:

Dot boom : marketing to baby boomers through meaningful online
engagement / Jonathan Boehman, David Weigelt.

Library of Congress Control Number: 2008943024

  1. Marketing.   2. Internet.   3. Baby boom generation.
  4. Consumer behavior.

ISBN: 0-9802118-3-2

Printed in the United States of America.

Cover design by Lisa Burroughs and Claire Urban
Photography by Ira Wexler
Interior design by Paul Fitzgerald
Illustrations by Claire Urban

Dedication

From Jonathan:

To David Baker, who pushed us out of our nest.
To David Weigelt, who took the leap with me.
To David Wolfe, who helped us to fly.
To the Immersion Active team, who helps us fly higher every day.
To our clients, who let us soar.
To my wife, Jess, who I'm lucky to fly back to every day.

From David:

To the most beautiful person I know — my wife. Stephanie, to the extent that this book represents my appreciation for the human spirit and the power of touching people's lives in meaningful ways, I thank you for twenty-four years of inspiration and on-the-job training. I love you very much.

Acknowledgements

This book represents the hard work and inspired ideas of twelve people. Truth be told, there is not an idea in this book that is owned solely by me or Jonathan. In many ways, the complexity of thought and diversity of ideas in this book are reflective of the team we are so blessed to work with on a daily basis.

Jonathan and I would like to acknowledge the contributions of Kathi Scharf and Joe Ford for melding the (often exclusive) humanistic and analytic ideas that make this book powerful; Claire Urban, Chris Boehman, and Lisa Burroughs for understanding that design isn't just how something looks but how it works; Matt Barrick and Darrin Maule, for appreciating how the technical side of our work has the potential to move people in either a positive or negative direction; Nathan Fitzgerald for helping us clarify our ideas; Caroline Lewis for creating the time for us to make this happen and insuring the quality of everything we do; Corey Grunewald for being a great "Intern Boy" and helping tirelessly with our research; and Lisa "Mamma" Hammer for being our token in-house boomer and keeping our billable ship afloat.

We would like to especially acknowledge one of our marketing coordinators, Erin Biles. As a journalism major straight out of school, she accepted our challenge to help us write this book and delivered beyond our expectations. The thoughtful words you are about to read are a testament to the potential for today's youth (Erin is a Millennial herself) to not only understand the needs of a mature consumer, but also to inspire them. Erin's words and input have given life to this book — for which we are eternally grateful.

In addition to the great team of professionals we work with, Jonathan and I are blessed to have several great mentors. As a consultant to our company and a revolutionary in the creative industry, David Baker changed the course of our business when, three years ago, he helped us define our niche with regard to the mature markets. The idea to write a book was his, but what he never told us was that the value lies in the journey — not the destination.

Finally, we want to thank the smartest marketer Jonathan and I have ever had the honor to be associated with, David Wolfe. As the author of several books, his title *Ageless Marketing* is the foundation of this book and everything we do as marketers. His intelligence and selflessness have turned a business specialty into a purpose that motivates us and our employees, have made our work disproportionately more effective, and have deepened our relationships with everyone with whom we work. To the man who taught us the value of understanding human behavior and the multiple stakeholder approach — we thank you most for teaching us the meaning of concinnity.

Contents

Foreword

When David Weigelt approached me about writing the forward to *Dot Boom,* I turned him down, demurred at first. My concern was one of self service, as the intellectual foundation of *Dot Boom* is a marketing model I designed called *Developmental Relationship Marketing.* But after several months of coaxing, David eased me over my concerns. At a minimum, he thought, it would serve readers' interests by validating his and Jonathan Boehman's interpretation of my work. So here I am, doing his bidding.

It is not a stretch to assert that the marketing agency that David and Jonathan founded, Immersion Active, stands alone. After all, it is the only U.S. marketing agency devoted *exclusively* to marketing to the 50-plus markets online. In similar respects, *Dot Boom* stands alone. As I write this, it is the only book devoted to online marketing to consumers age 50 and older.

Actually, I have encouraged David and Jonathan to lower the floor of their market universe to age 40. After reading the first several chapters, you will understand why. But to summarize, a shift in a person's life course generally takes place around age 40, rather than age 50. Provided we're not still battling for satisfaction of our basic needs, we experience something of a personal paradigm shift around the onset of midlife. Typically, our worldview mellows. Life is less etched in black and white than how we once saw it, and we begin devoting more of our psychic energies to giving and being, rather than getting and having. Of course, not everyone travels this path of personal transformation. However, the vast majority of us experience personal transformation in some form, which is in accordance with the theories of many adult development luminaries, from Carl Jung and Abraham Maslow to Erik Erikson and Claire Graves.

Dot Boom creatively recognizes that the onset of midlife changes people's worldviews, values, and aspirations. In doing so, it describes something that may come as a surprise to those who once predicted that boomers would enter their retirement years with adolescent self-absorption: Boomers no longer deserve the "Me Generation" label. They have become the "We Generation" — striving to rise above the self to leave the world a little better than they found it. This has fomented radical changes in consumer behavior. The ethos of narcissism and materialism that dominated Madison Avenue culture for most of the 20th century is in ebb tide. *Dot Boom* accurately reflects this critical change in the contemporary *zeitgeist* better than almost any other book I've read. And I read a lot of books.

Of everything I've read over the years, few rise to a level of scholarship that supports the author's propositions. Authors avoid the marks of critical thinking, depending instead on opinions and anecdotes more than on solidly grounded propositions. Dumbing down books in hopes of elevating sales is a literary statement that I think my profession carries a bit too far.

Publishers tell authors, "Don't get too theoretical" — whatever *that* means. I learned what that means to the former editorial head of a Doubleday division. After she turned one of my books down, my agent asked me to call her and personally plead my case. She got right to the point — she liked the topic, liked my writing, but thought my book was too complex for marketers.

"Leave out the theory, make it simpler, fill it with numbered lists of things to do and things not to do. Don't get into a long discussion about why an idea is a good idea. Just say it's good and move on. The reader considers you the expert, so don't spend a lot of time defending yourself." Although that conversation took place about 15 years ago, I vividly remember it to this day.

I pleaded: "But without a well-grounded intellectual foundation, how will readers know that I'm not selling hogwash?"

"You don't have to worry about that. Marketers don't really care *why* something works. They only want to know *what* works." Then she came up with a depressing statement about the intellectual competence of marketers.

"Mr. Wolfe," she said, "I don't know about you, but I haven't met many marketers who are all that smart. You need to simplify your book for us to be interested."

David manages to write in a breezy, accessible style without dumbing down the sophisticated ideas developed in *Dot Boom*. When he proposes that something will work, he tells readers why, with solid intellectual backing. But he does something else that makes *Dot Boom* a refreshing marketing book.

We've all heard the old saw about how giving a man a fish feeds him for a day, but teaching him how to fish will enable him to eat for a lifetime. David and Jonathan teach readers how to fish. They give them intellectual tools that enable readers to write their own prescriptions for solving problems.

Publishers tell us that marketers want solutions. But I think that any marketer worth his salt generally prefers learning how to design their own solutions than to be given a fixed answer designed by someone else. A smart marketer knows that no two problems are quite alike. John Wanamaker, who opened the first U.S. department store in 1869, memorialized this condition when he famously complained, "Half the money I spend on advertising is wasted; the trouble is I don't know which half." More than 140 years have passed since he uttered those words, and we still do not have *the* answer to his problem.

And 140 years from now, marketers will still be trying to find the Unified Theory of Advertising that reduces customers to the certainties of cause-and-effect models of marketplace behavior. However, if human behavior could be reduced to such expressions of certainty, the ancient case against freewill would be closed forever. The answers to marketing's greatest questions will not be found in stimulus-response formulations of consumer behavior.

Belgian chemist Nobel Laureate Ilya Prigogine wrote a book a few years back, *The End of Certainty*. In it, he laments the seeming obsession in Western culture and science with the pursuit of certainty. He alleges that more often than we'd all like to admit, certainty is an illusion. Probabilities and uncertainties rule the world — not the laws of statistics and mechanistic cause-and-effect or stimulus-response determinism.

Marketers have generally relied more heavily on numbers than on tenets of human behavior to guide them through the marketing universe. The bias should run in the opposite direction — marketers should rely more on tenets of behavior than on statistical arrays and data points in trying to divine consumer behavior prospectively. However, the wisdom of this bias was long concealed by the marketplace dominance of youth over the past six or seven decades. The market behavior of the young reflects group values more strongly than individual values. Once you have an idea of what the group will do, you have a pretty good idea of what the individual will do. With older consumers — who are now the majority — you have to figure out what the individual is predisposed toward doing. After you've done that you *may* have a pretty good idea of what the group (if there is one) will do.

Despite their vaunted expressions of individualism, youth exults conformity — in fact, youth demands it. Entry to social groups that are important to fulfilling one's needs and aspirations depends on conforming to a group's worldviews and values. Older people tend to regard conformity as a compromise of self-expression. As they move into and through the second half of life, peer influence wanes. Released from the mindless clutches of conformity, they become subject to a broader spectrum of influences than when they were young. This makes their behavior less predictable, hence a greater challenge to those who see aging boomers as merely an older version of their younger selves.

Not to worry, say researchers. We'll survey aging boomers just like we do tweens and teens. We'll let them tell us what they want and don't want. They will inform us as to their worldviews, values, and aspirations. And we'll believe in drawing statistical pictures of them based on their own testimony.

Bzzzz. Wrong.

The older the consumer population, the more likely the results of survey style research are seriously flawed. Little consumer research in older markets takes into account the differences in how older brains process information. For example, answers to scaled questions like "Strongly Agree to Strongly Disagree" often lead to flawed conclusions because older minds generally operate with greater sensitivity to context than they did when they were younger.

Often, when encountering such questions, older minds want to say, "it depends" or "sometimes but not always." In not being able to so condition their responses, older respondents often pick one that seems closest to the truth on *that* day and *that* day only.

Metrics dominate market research, including readouts of marketing results. However, much of what is measured matters little and much of what matters a lot never gets measured — or as Einstein said, "Not everything that can be counted counts, and not everything that counts can be counted."

David and Jonathan respect Einstein's wisdom in Chapter 7 when they explore the topic of "Meaningful Online Engagement." This chapter is where these two leap ahead, taking readers from the inevitable distortions of psychographics to the true-to-life renderings of customers as they work their way through their decisions, often contradicting what they (or their surrogates) once told researchers in surveys or focus groups.

"We live in an uncertain world" is a rather tired cliché. However, that does not make the thought it expresses any less true. I submit that marketing is an underperforming profession, and is so because too many in the field — beginning in academe — view customers as stimulus-response mechanisms whose behavior can ultimately be accounted for with all the certainty of a cannonball's trajectory. But there are huge differences between the physics of objects hurtling through space and time and the behavior of people in the marketplace.

It is time that the marketing profession renounce the illusory certainty of Newtonian physics. It needs to recalibrate its functions around the idea of discovering the behavioral principles that underlie consumers' decisions. It needs to reorient its practitioners to the inevitable uncertainties that attend the freewill choices in the marketplace.

David and Jonathan manage a renunciation of the myth that although meteorologists often miss their predictions of weather behavior, market researchers can get consumer's behavior down cold, given enough money, data points, and computer power.

One of my most delightful moments in reading this highly engaging book was coming across their new definition of marketing. It is elegant in its shimmering simplicity. Before getting to that definition, read the definition approved in 2007 by the board of directors of the American Marketing Association:

> "Marketing is the activity, set of institutions, and processes for creating, communicating, delivering, and exchanging offerings that have value for customers, clients, partners, and society at large."

The essence of marketing according to Immersion Active is "the exchange of information within a topic." It may take a few moments to blink away the marketer-centric bearing of AMA's definition to develop a broader and more profound view of marketing. In the Developmental Relationship Marketing model, marketplaces are viewed as cultural ecosystems that exist to meet the demands of countless nodes of interdependency that exist among participants in the system. Keep in mind; ecology involves the study of exchange relationships. Fundamental to any exchange between interdependent parties is information. Thus, the appropriateness of Boehman and Weigelt's definition of marketing.

Few business books — especially marketing books — are worth reading all the way through. Most get the job done in two or three chapters. To compensate, they do variations on their original themes until they've got enough pages to fill book. My only disappointment in reading *Dot Boom* (in its entirety) is that *it's not long enough.* I hope you have the same delightful experience.

David B. Wolfe, co-author of Ageless Marketing and Firms
of Endearment
Reston, Virginia
November 30, 2008

Preface

On Friday, October 3, 2008, Jonathan and I, along with four of our Immersion Active team members, were sitting in a lecture room in New York City, anxiously awaiting our first presentation on some of the points from this book. Our presentation's title — "Online Campaign Optimization: Influencing Boomers through Meaningful Online Engagement" — was a mouthful, but we were confident the subject matter would resonate with the noteworthy group of boomer-focused marketers the Focalyst Executive Forum drew.

As the presentation before ours was about to begin, one of our employees rushed over to our table. "The House approved the bailout," she whispered, explaining that she had overheard the news from an attendee who had been monitoring her BlackBerry.

Politics (and a fleeting twinge of jealousy that our company doesn't manufacture wooden arrows) aside, I wasn't surprised. Even before Congress passed the "Emergency Economic Stabilization Act of 2008" (better know as *the* bailout), we knew that this conference was not going to be a typical "boomers spend, SPEND, *SPEND!*" event. From CMOs to entrepreneurs, we all were facing the sobering reality of an uncertain economy. Yet, here we all were, attending an event focused on connecting with the *wealthiest* generation in the history of the United States.

As the preceding group came to a close, each of us approached the stage with thoughts not on the 30-minute presentation we were about to deliver, but on the future of our nation's economy and how our company's clients and, more importantly, the boomers were going to react.

Later, after the conference came to a close and as our train was departing New York's Penn Station, I thought about how marketers were going to adapt. We all know marketing is often first in line to be affected by uncertain times (from tightened budgets to agency consolidations to layoffs). And in tough times, the easiest (and usually most common) way for marketers to adapt is to become protective of our turf and reactionary in our tactics.

But, I asked myself, with terms like "crisis," "recession," and even "depression" being thrown around like warm-up pitches at Camden Yards, is that really how marketing should respond?

The conclusion I reached as our train barreled through Philadelphia was exactly the opposite: In tough times, it is our opportunity as marketers to shine. Our job as communication professionals is not simply to market to people. Our job is to move people, to inspire them, and to help them process their lives. Thinking about our role within the context of this new economic reality reaffirmed to me the importance of understanding what truly motivates consumers and the need to develop marketing campaigns that proactively engage them in authentic and meaningful relationships.

That is what our company aims to do. When Jonathan and I founded Immersion Active ten years ago, we were driven by the need to create meaningful and enriching interactive experiences online. Our goal was to engage our clients' target audiences in the most relevant manner possible.

Early on, we recognized that a higher level of engagement begins and ends with a better understanding of the user. By immersing ourselves in the user experience, we realized that taking advantage of the ever-changing nature of interactive media required more of a focus. This realization pushed us to dedicate Immersion Active to the 50-plus markets — a consumer group that is the Web's largest and fastest-growing constituency[1], yet remains the most underserved by online marketing.

Initially, some of our industry peers questioned us for such a focus. Now, some of those same skeptics are once again raising their red flags (or white may be more appropriate) in our direction. They think that the boomers are to blame for our country's problems. Others are suggesting that with their retirement funds melting away, boomers and their needs will just shrivel up and disappear.

There's no denying that boomers, and most Americans for that matter, are currently re-evaluating their finances and will need to make adjustments. That said, it is our belief that the needs of this large, aging demographic will continue to drive the market for many years to come.

Always the optimists, most boomers will not only find ways to meet their base needs, but also find a way to maintain the lifestyles they have become accustomed to. I recently read one journalist's assertion that "despite the current doom-and-gloom about the state of the housing market, retirement, and savings, experts believe boomers will be able to stay the course and at the same time change the way marketers target consumers[2]."

We agree. Baby boomers will continue to be the most powerful consumers in the marketplace. Jonathan and I see this already in our work at Immersion Active. At a time when a lot of agencies and marketers are struggling, our company continues to be blessed with plenty of clients whose focus on targeting older adults is helping them thrive.

To help our clients make the most of any tough situation, we as marketers need to focus our efforts on connecting with these powerful consumers by showing them how our brands can continue to help them.

As marketers ourselves, Jonathan and I also recognize the growing need for better return on investments in challenging times. More and more, the Internet is providing the most efficient and effective ways to achieve these results, especially with boomer consumers. In fact, 72 percent of online retailers said that online channels are better suited than offline channels to withstand an economic slowdown, mainly because consumers on a budget shop online for convenience and better values[3].

That's where the strategies in *Dot Boom* come in. The philosophies, principles, and techniques explained throughout this book will enable marketers to successfully, and repeatedly, deliver effective online campaigns targeting mature adults (as they have for us).

Dot Boom: Marketing to Baby Boomers through Meaningful Online Engagement provides insight into the baby boomer markets, their online motivations, online behavior, and online preferences. As you read *Dot Boom*, you'll gain a deeper understanding of what baby boomers want and need from an Internet marketing campaign. You'll also explore a framework you can use to create these campaigns in a replicable, effective manner.

To begin, you'll learn David Wolfe's Developmental Relationship Marketing (DRM) concepts to discover what motivates older consumers' purchasing decisions, especially in relation to the Internet. Engaging older consumers online is not simply about understanding their *user* behavior, but understanding the biological and psychological motivators behind that behavior. You can then use that knowledge to create better online connections between your brand and your target audience through relevant messaging and imagery.

Later, we'll focus on a process to develop campaigns that encompass the variety of ways in which boomers engage with your brand online. Engagement is a marketing buzzword that's been getting a lot of attention lately, but so far, Jonathan and I have been unable to find an engagement definition that 1) works well for boomers, and 2) allows us to determine why a campaign is successful.

That's why we've developed our own, boomer-specific definition of engagement — Meaningful Online Engagement. It is a definition that helps us methodically identify what works and what doesn't, so we are able to replicate our successful campaigns again and again. This definition, as described in the second half of *Dot Boom*, will give you the framework to create an effective engagement strategy and to insert your brand into boomers' digital lives in a powerful way.

In first embarking on *Dot Boom*, Jonathan and I decided that we wanted readers to walk away with actionable ideas on how to better connect with baby boomers online. Now, more than ever, marketers need a better way to reach these dynamic, lucrative consumers — none of whom fit neatly into traditional demographic segments. Today's marketing professionals require online strategies that are different. *Dot Boom* breaks down those strategies and provides guidance on how to effectively and efficiently market to baby boomers online.

As we all continue to adapt to our nation's (and world's) changing economy, I'm comforted when I think about October 3. That night, as I exited the train in Baltimore (our final destination) and watched my bleary-eyed co-workers sleepily stumble onto the platform, I thought about our book. The Focalyst Executive Forum was the first time Jonathan and I unveiled *Dot Boom* to our industry peers. And after that train ride, amidst all of the uncertainty our nation faced, I realized that we had a message that resonated. More important, we have a book that can be part of the solution.

Happy reading.

A note from Jonathan:

When David and I began writing, we consistently stumbled over the "voice" of *Dot Boom*. Taking us back to grammar school, we debated first person singular, first person plural, second person omniscient…you get the idea.

We first decided on the almighty "we." We're business partners and co-authors. It only made sense to write from both of our perspectives. Unfortunately, the end result was a bit confusing.

Then, to preserve the clarity of our thoughts and ideas, David and I decided that it should be written in a singular voice. So what you will be reading is in the voice of David, not me.

Do I feel slighted? Do I feel any less part of this book — a project two years in the making? Absolutely not. This book was an enlightening endeavor for both of us. And besides, if you ever meet the two of us, you'll see that our decision definitely reflects the dynamic of our partnership. (David talks. A lot.)

Enjoy!

Section 1:
Challenging Conventional Marketing

There's no denying the impact, even from a mere demographic standpoint, that the baby boomer generation has had (and is continuing to have!) on the United States. Their size and influence, and the subsequent focus the media has placed on them throughout their lives, have made them the nucleus of our cultural center, ultimately driving — and in their later years shaping — the societal norms that other generations follow.

By looking at boomers in the news today, it's apparent that they are not slowing down as they reach retirement. They remain powerful and influential consumers, both online and off, and they demand significant marketing attention. Their economic clout, in combination with the ever-evolving nature of the Internet, requires a much-needed re-evaluation of conventional marketing strategies.

In this first section of *Dot Boom*, we'll explore the promise that online marketing to baby boomers holds and the problems marketers must overcome before truly connecting with that potential.

1

Chapter 1:
The Promise of Marketing to Boomers Online

"When I get older, losing my hair, many years from now... Will you still need me, will you still feed me, when I'm 64?"

— The Beatles, *"When I'm 64"*

Such an upbeat tune from Sgt. Pepper's Lonely Hearts Club Band has never been so relevant to the generation that came of age worshipping John, Paul, George, and Ringo. Why? Because despite boomers' reputation as a force to be reckoned with, many of today's institutions, organizations, and businesses still fail to understand what truly motivates these older adults' behavior. This lack of understanding is especially pervasive within the marketing industry.

Traditional marketing tactics and techniques have focused on the 18- to 35-year-old demographic because when boomers were in that age range, they represented a huge consumer majority (the likes of which had never been seen before). However, now that those same 18- to 35-year-olds have moved on to a new season of life, marketers have failed to transition with them. For the first time in history, the majority of the United States population is over age 40[4] — and adults over 40 think and act much differently than their younger counterparts. They go about fulfilling their needs differently, making their purchasing behavior unique. As a result, traditional marketing approaches are simply not effective with this consumer majority because traditional marketing lacks the perspective required to understand the needs of an aging adult.

In other words (and my Fantasy Football buddies will shudder upon hearing me use this phrase), *marketing needs a makeover.* That's the only way we, as marketers, can effectively reach today's older consumer majority.

But where to start? Before delving into the issues surrounding marketing to boomers, especially online, let's take a quick look at the boomers themselves.

Baby [bey-bee] *noun*: an infant or very young child[5].

Boom [boom] *verb*: to move with a resounding rush or great impetus; to progress, grow, or flourish vigorously[6].

Baby boom [bey-bee boom] *noun*: a period of sharp increase in the birthrate, as that in the U.S. following World War II[7].

Behind the Boom

Baby boomers are one of the largest generational cohorts the United States has ever seen. While the first boomers will turn 64 in 2010, the last of this 78-million-strong cohort will not reach that age until the year 2028. With birth years spanning 18 years (1946 to 1964), the baby boomers will be an important consumer group for many years to come.

In fact, according to data from the U.S. Census Bureau (who I'll reference often in this book), people over the age of 40 now account for more than 60 percent of all adults, numbering 138 million. That is compared to just 91 million adults under age 40. What's even more significant is that the gap between older and younger adults will continue to grow. Between now and 2025, the younger adult crowd will grow by approximately seven-tenths of 1 percent, adding 6.9 million to that group. However, the number of adults over 40 will increase by more than 21 percent, meaning that there will be almost 30 million more adults over the age of 40 in 2025 than there are today.

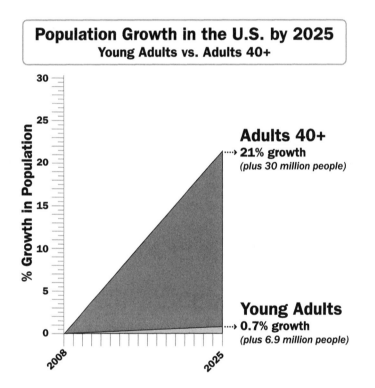

Boomers in the United States are more racially and ethnically diverse than previous generations, with almost 20 percent of today's boomers being members of minority groups[8]. They are also the most educated, with almost 90 percent of baby boomers graduating from high school, versus only 68 percent of their parents[9]. Boomers are even slightly more likely to have a college degree than members of the younger Generation X[10].

And, currently, boomers are experiencing more significant life events, simultaneously, than any other generation. Today's boomers are raising toddlers, becoming grandparents, caring for their aging parents, getting married, getting divorced, retiring, going back to school, starting new careers, and more. This unique combination of life events makes it especially difficult to segment or group boomers using traditional demographic approaches.

Meet the Boomers

Clearly, boomers are not one big, homogenous group. In turn, I could never attempt to create a prototypical boomer that represents them all. But in an effort to bring the concepts, theories, and practices of this book to life, I'll refer to three specific boomers throughout the first two sections of this book. Let me introduce you to Mary, Robert, and Carol, all based on three real boomers. (I've simply changed names to protect the innocent.)

Mary

Mary is a 55-year-old mother of three. Her oldest child, a 24-year-old woman, recently moved back in with Mary, bringing her 5-year-old daughter (Mary's granddaughter) with her. Mary's oldest son is 21 and also lives at home while he attends trade school. Her youngest son is a senior in high school. Mary has always been very active in all of her children's (and grandchild's) lives, attending their sporting events, supporting the booster club, and driving them wherever they needed to go.

Mary's mother died last year and her father lives about five hours away. She has close ties with her family and tries to get home whenever she can. She often worries about her father living alone and wonders if she and her siblings will soon need to care for him.

Mary works the night shift at the local hospital as a pediatric nurse. Her husband (of 30 years) works as a project manager for a computer software company. His long commute is taking a heavy toll on him and he is talking about wanting to change careers or find something closer to home (despite the obligatory pay cut).

Robert

Robert is a 53-year-old man with two children who are about to finish college. One goes to school in Texas and the other in California. About five years ago, Robert sold his printing business, which he had owned for almost 20 years, and decided to retire in his home state of Massachusetts. His retirement only lasted about a year. Then, because of boredom and, more important, a need to finance his children's college education, he took a job with the local school system in its printing office.

Robert spends a significant amount of time looking after his elderly mother. She recently broke her hip in a fall and has been in and out of a nursing facility as she recovers. Robert has been forced to figure out all the intricacies of Medicare and health insurance in a relatively short period of time. When she is not in nursing care, Robert's mother lives in her own home, which is about 20 minutes from Robert's house.

When he is not working or caring for his mother, Robert stays active in the community, primarily through the local high school. There, despite the fact that his youngest child graduated six years ago, Robert coaches the local lacrosse team, is president of the school's booster club, and runs the concession stand at athletic events year round.

Carol

Carol is a 60-year-old woman with three grown children. All three are married, have their own children, and live within two hours of Carol's home. Carol was married to her high school sweetheart for 30 years before they divorced 10 years ago. Since then, Carol remarried a man who has a 28-year-old daughter of his own (who is also divorced) and an autistic grandson. Family is extremely important to Carol and she talks to each of her children at least three or four times a week.

Carol worked as a secretary for about 15 years but quit working when she remarried. She has also always been very active in her church and in community organizations such as the Friends of the Library.

In recent years, Carol has started to suffer from a variety of health conditions including fibromyalgia and celiac disease (an allergy to wheat products). Both of these conditions make it difficult for Carol to drive, get out of the house, and do many physical activities. In addition, her husband, who is three years younger than she, works more than 60 hours per week, meaning Carol is home alone much of the time.

While baby boomers have and probably always will be grouped together simply because of the high birth rate between

1946 and 1964, don't make the mistake of thinking that all boomers are alike just because of their age. Woodstock may have been huge, but did all 78 million baby boomers attend? Not a chance. In fact, a boomer who is age 50 today was only 11 years old during that historic music festival.

And despite the stereotype that boomers have an affinity for radical social and political change, boomers did not lead many of our country's definitive movements, such as Civil Rights, feminism, and the protest against the Vietnam War. Rev. Dr. Martin Luther King, Jr. and Bob Dylan were members of the Silent Generation and Betty Friedan (who wrote *The Feminine Mystique*) was a member of the GI Generation. In fact, a study by Chadwick Martin Bailey found that only 15 percent of boomers claim to have participated in demonstrations or protests.

However, social consciousness has risen to the top of boomers' charts as they've aged. So while they aren't racing for the rallies, picket signs in hands, as consumers, baby boomers are very responsive to companies that maintain a sense of social consciousness and give back[11]. Boomers are also going green faster than younger generations. Both of these trends reflect boomers' maturing psyches, acceptance of their age, and desire to leave a legacy behind them.

But the drive to leave the world a better place is not unique to today's boomers. These socially conscious desires are largely driven by deep-seated biological and psychological needs that are shared by all humans as we grow older. Today's boomers may be exhibiting them most markedly, but it was these same needs that also drove King, Dylan, and Freidan in the '60s.

Boomer Bucks

Let's get down to what really matters to marketers: "Boomer Bucks" (as my 11-year-old daughter likes to call them). In 2005, baby boomers possessed three-quarters of the nation's financial assets and an estimated $1 trillion in *annual* disposable income[12]. And despite the stock market declines (as of the publication of this book), boomers still control more wealth than their younger counterparts.

According to the Bureau of Labor Statistics, 75 percent of adults age 45 to 54 owned their own homes in 2006 (compared to only 50 percent of 25 to 34 year olds)[13]. And while housing values may have decreased in recent years, home ownership still provides for a greater overall net worth.

In addition, the average boomer household earned almost $20,000 more per year in 2006 than younger households[14]. And older workers are generally the most highly employed. In September 2008, the unemployment rate for 24 to 35 year olds was 6.1 percent while the unemployment rate for 45 to 54 year olds was only 4.4 percent[15]. (The lowest, 4.1 percent, was for adults age 55 and older[16].)

What's more, boomers outspend their younger consumer counterparts in almost all areas. The Bureau of Labor Statistics[17] reported that in 2006, younger boomers (age 45 to 54) outspend younger adults (age 25 to 34) in all major areas:

	Age 25 to 34	Age 45 to 54
Income before taxes	$57,208	$77,043
Homeowners	50 percent	75 percent
Average annual expenditures	$47,582	$57,563
Food at home	$6,104	$7,328
Food away from home	$2,918	$3,292
Housing	$17,139	$18,377
Clothing	$2,152	$2,176

Transportation	$9,047	$10,111
Healthcare	$1,652	$2,757
Entertainment	$2,237	$2,770
Personal care products	$547	$696
Education	$710	$1,736
Insurance and pensions	$5,252	$7,346
Cash contributions	$1,070	$2,118
Miscellaneous	$615	$971

As previously stated, the before-tax income of adults age 45 to 54 is almost $20,000 more than adults age 25 to 34. In 2006, there were 24.7 million young boomer (age 45 to 54) households compared to only 20.1 million young adult (age 25 to 34) households. Through simple math, you can reach the conclusion that young boomer households have a *combined difference* of more than $92 billion annually.

Another significant aspect of boomer spending, aside from the sheer size of the generation, is that today, the majority of boomers are in or entering their peak earning years, as peak earning age is generally considered to be between the ages of 45 and 54[18].

Boomers Online

Demographics indicate that boomers are a highly educated, diverse consumer group ready to connect with your brand. And boomers are ready to connect with your brand *online*. One misconception sometimes associated with boomers is that because they did not grow up with the Internet, they do not go online. Baby boomers are, in fact, the Web's largest constituency, making up more than 30 percent of the United States' 195.3 million Internet users[19]. It should come as no surprise that adults over the age of 50 are the Internet's fastest-growing group[20].

In 2011, the number of boomers who use the Internet at least once a month will reach 63.7 million. In addition, "83.2 percent of U.S. baby boomers will use the Internet regularly in 2011, up from 75 percent in 2006[21]." And during a typical week, 90 percent of boomers (who already use the Internet) read and send email and 86 percent surf the Internet[22].

It's important for you to know that baby boomers are willing to spend their money online, as well as offline. On average, baby boomers spend $7 billion online annually[23]. And weekly, 77 percent of baby boomers purchase products online, (a mere 1 percent less than Generation X — a statistical dead heat — and 24 percent more than Generation Y)[24].

In a 2007 study, Forrester Research concluded that older boomers (between the ages of 52 and 62) spend the most money online[25]. That same study also found that while younger generations (X and Y) are more likely to have recently purchased something online, more than three-quarters of all baby boomers regularly buy online[26]. Consider the following figures[27]:

Baby boomers have the largest annual household income, so it's logical to conclude that they would spend more than younger generations who make less. But when members of each generation were asked how much they currently spend and are planning to spend online, the boomer response was double.

- **Generation Y (age 18 to 27)**
  - Spent online in the past three months: $429
  - Expected to spend online in the next three months: $313
- **Generation X (age 28 to 41)**
  - Spent online in the past three months: $558
  - Expected to spend online in the next three months: $451

- **Baby boomers (age 42 to 62)**
    - Spent online in the past three months: $1,150
    - Expected to spend online in the next three months: $1,260

Further emphasizing these findings, eMarketer observes that, "boomers wield enormous economic clout and are increasingly turning to online and mobile channels for a variety of needs, including e-commerce, financial services, travel, entertainment, health and wellness information, news, and user-generated content[28]."

Boomers aren't just buying online either. They are using the Internet to research both online and offline purchases. According to a 2006 study conducted for FH Boom, baby boomers cite the Internet as the most important source of information when they make a major marketing purchase, such as automobiles or appliances[29]. Frankly, I've found that most boomers cannot imagine life without the Internet. During the summer of 2007, Immersion Active conducted "man-on-the-street" interviews with baby boomers in my hometown of Frederick, Maryland. We posed a simple question: "What would you do without the Internet?"

The answers ranged from sighs of disbelief to nervous laughter. And throughout the significantly wide range of answers, not one of the boomers interviewed could fathom living without the Internet. The most poignant answer came from a lively, professional woman, whose face twisted in disgust as she answered: "I would have to go to the… *Yellow Pages*? Or to… [sigh] I don't even know. And I'm not young, and my mother is 79, and she does the same thing."

View interviews online
www.dotboombook.com/boomer_videos

The Internet offers a plethora of opportunities to reach and engage boomers (because clearly, the phone book is not going to cut it). It's just a matter of sorting through the myriad of online opportunities to determine the best way to connect with these consumers. This process begins with an understanding of *how* boomers are interacting with online media.

The Web Goes "Boom"

According to a study conducted by ThirdAge*, the top three reasons baby boomers spend time online are to seek out information (92 percent), to stay in touch with friends and family (92 percent), and to shop online (73 percent)[30]. Sharing information, or word of mouth, is especially important for boomers. On average, most baby boomers are asked for product or service recommendations about 90 times per year and close to 90 percent of boomers who were asked to give advice gave it to their fellow boomers. Practically all boomers consider their family and friends to be their most trusted sources of information[31]. What's most relevant is the growing use of the Internet for word-of-mouth interaction, as nearly half (45 percent) of all boomer word-of-mouth recommendations are made online[32].

Baby boomers are often referred to as the "TV generation," as they were the first generation to come of age with television in the home. Online, video is gaining "prominence as a source of news, entertainment, sports, and user-generated content, among other media types[33]" for boomers. Our own research found that this sentiment also translates into an affinity for rich media content, especially when it's used to assist or entertain the user.

Boomers are also beginning to bridge the gap between the ever-expanding channels of social media. The Pew Internet and American

Please note that multiple responses were allowed.

Life Project concluded that boomers are more like younger age groups than they are like seniors when it comes to user-generated content, being more likely to pursue a broader range of activities online and to experiment with newer online pursuits, such as blogs and social networks.

When boomers do participate in social media, they are currently more likely to be passive participants, reading blogs and reviews as opposed to actually posting a comment and blogging themselves. In fact, in a given week, 27 percent of boomers read blogs, while only 7 percent actually blog[34].

But even though boomers are closer in usage to younger users than to seniors, they are not adopting social networking (MySpace, Facebook, and the like) as rapidly as their younger counterparts. However, looking forward, eMarketer predicts that more than 50 percent of the U.S. adult population will use social networks by 2011, compared to 37 percent in 2008[35].

What's important to for us to understand from these statistics is that, while boomers may lag behind younger age groups in their adoption of a specific technology, boomers will generally follow suit soon afterwards. Consider these trends:

- Although their Instant Messaging (IM) usage has not nearly reached the saturation levels common among teenagers and younger adults, it is rising in popularity among boomers. This trend is most likely driven by boomers' desire to keep in touch with their younger family members.
- 79.5 percent of boomers own mobile phones, but their daily mobile Internet access is similar to younger users — across all generations it's less than 5 percent[36]. (However, I expect this to rapidly change as devices like Apple's iPhone and the Google phone become more mainstream.)

- Boomers, like the majority of all Internet users, say they do not use RSS[37]. (However, I should note that most users — regardless of age — often do not even realize when they are consuming RSS content. They simply know that their news headlines are being updated.)

A general misconception might be that older adults' slightly slower adoption rate makes them poor candidates for digital marketing. But it's important to keep in mind that current adoption rates do not necessarily reflect the true potential of any given technology or technique.

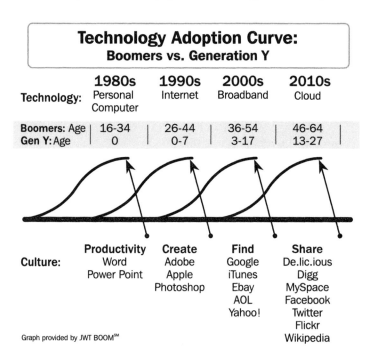

Technology Adoption Curve:
Boomers vs. Generation Y

Technology:	1980s Personal Computer	1990s Internet	2000s Broadband	2010s Cloud
Boomers: Age	16-34	26-44	36-54	46-64
Gen Y: Age	0	0-7	3-17	13-27

Culture:	Productivity Word Power Point	Create Adobe Apple Photoshop	Find Google iTunes Ebay AOL Yahoo!	Share De.lic.ious Digg MySpace Facebook Twitter Flickr Wikipedia

Graph provided by JWT BOOM℠

In fact, current adoption rates show just the opposite, exemplified by the above technology prediction curve. For example, boomers may have been slower to initially adopt email or use search engines, but today, email is the primary way boomers stay in touch with friends and family online. In addition, search is one of the most popular ways boomers seek out information online. On any given day, 46.5 percent of Generation X and Y use search, with boomers not far behind — 38 percent use a search engine daily[38].

Because boomers tend to follow suit with the technology adoption of younger generations, marketers may be able to leverage this slower adoption rate to predict future technology usage more accurately. Marketers can also prepare for an oncoming shift in usage by evaluating the current state of younger demographics.

Where, What, and Why?

Another common misconception about boomers' Internet usage is that they are going to different places than other age groups. Actually, our research finds that the places they are going are not that different from younger audiences, from categories of websites to specific Web properties. (For more on our research, see the appendix titled "Where Are They Online?")

So is there any value in knowing where baby boomers are online? Of course, especially for the sake of media planning. But just knowing *where* boomers are online and even *what* they are doing isn't enough. Effectively crafting boomer marketing campaigns also depends on understanding *why* they are online. We need to understand what is motivating their behavior and how to engage with them. We can then leverage a deeper understanding of boomer consumers to actually *influence* their actions.

One of the things Jonathan and I wrestled with when we began studying the boomer markets was figuring out what these consumers were doing differently online that warranted a special approach. What we quickly learned is that, at first blush, where boomers were going and what boomers were doing online did not seem that unique. But beyond the easily observed there are some very important differences in how they go about making decisions online. Herein lies what we believe to be one of the greatest opportunities on the Web.

So where do we begin? With a need to do things differently.

The Take-Away

For the first time in history, the majority of the U.S. population is over age 40, a direct result of the aging boomers. When it comes to this new consumer majority's spending habits, they are vibrant, informed, and are in or about to enter their peak spending years. In addition, boomers are experiencing numerous concurrent life events like no other generation before, giving them more reasons to use the Internet — creating all the more potential for marketers to extend their brand's influence to effectively connect with them online.

Chapter 2:
The Need to Do Things Differently

"Gonna change my way of thinking, make myself a different set of rules. Gonna put my good foot forward, and stop being influenced by fools."

> – Bob Dylan, *"Gonna Change My Way of Thinking"*

As I suggested in Chapter 1, we need to reconsider some of today's conventional marketing strategies if we want to successfully engage boomer consumers online. It's time for that makeover.

Boomers (and older adults in general) see life through different lenses than younger adults and have become disenchanted with traditional marketing approaches. A recent poll conducted by Harris Interactive found that nearly two-thirds of people believe that television programming and advertising is targeted at those under age 40[39]. And, according to a study by TV Land, more than one-third of boomers, representing more than 25 million people, are dissatisfied with the current state of marketing[40].

Advertising messages continually disenfranchise boomer consumers in a number of ways. First, marketing messages fail to connect with boomers as the vibrant consumers they are today. Advertising is an industry dominated by young professionals, whose naturally biased views of older adults are often reflected in the marketing messages they create for boomers.

In addition, today's marketing approaches often deliver fragmented, transaction-obsessed messages that fail to understand the factors that drive human behavior. Sometimes marketers deliver successful campaigns (which encompass the appropriate mix of creative, strategy, and technology), but then fail to understand why it worked so well. What's more is that they lack a repeatable, systematic framework to reproduce it.

In other words, conventional marketing lacks three key ingredients:

- A deeper understanding of human behavior

- A holistic measurement of marketing effectiveness

- A framework for replicable success

Let's take a quick look at each ingredient now and then explore them in greater depth throughout the rest of *Dot Boom*.

Understanding Human Behavior

Baby boomers have and probably always will be grouped together simply because of the high birth rate between 1946 and 1964 — but don't make the mistake of thinking that all boomers are alike just because of their similar birth years. At this stage in their lives, boomers are experiencing more significant life events simultaneously than any other generation. It is this characteristic that makes targeting boomers both lucrative (change equals opportunity) and difficult.

The fact is that regardless of our life events, and to some extent, regardless of our age, *all humans* have certain basic needs we are trying to fulfill[41]. And it is the drive to meet these needs that motivates our behavior. We can't help it. It's natural. However, people of different ages will go about fulfilling their needs in different ways. You, me, and everyone we know will make conscious decisions about how we meet our needs, which are often influenced by our age.

By determining what needs a person is trying to fulfill and showing how your brand can help meet those needs (in whatever manner consumers are trying to fulfill them), you can more effectively target today's boomers. It is this aspect of the aging boomers that makes a unique marketing approach critical.

This approach, called Developmental Relationship Marketing or DRM (developed by human behavior expert David Wolfe), helps us, as marketers, reach aging consumers on a deeper, more meaningful level. By understanding the most basic motivators of behavior, the marketing messages you develop appeal to consumers' basic human needs, not simply their life events, age, or actions.

In Section 2 of this book, we'll explore the DRM approach and present you with proven methods to help you move toward addressing the *motivation* behind the boomer consumer's buying behavior.

As important as it is to understand human behavior and consumer motivators, effective online marketing requires more. It requires a different way to measure and monitor the success of our efforts.

Holistically Measuring Marketing Effectiveness

For years, marketers have lived and died by metrics such as cost-per-sale, cost-per-acquisition, and cost-per-lead. Quite frankly, the beauty and the bane of the Internet is that it has made it possible to add even more measurements to this list (such as impressions, hits, clicks, and conversions) and allows these metrics to be monitored more precisely. Unfortunately, the very things that have helped marketers prove their value has also led to a decrease in marketing's overall effectiveness.

When comparing trends in overall productivity costs for U.S.-based corporations, marketing is the only operational area where costs have risen over time while effectiveness has decreased. In other words, while the manufacturing and administration departments have generally been accomplishing more with less, marketers are actually spending *more* money and achieving *less-effective* results. Why? Because marketing, especially online marketing, has continued to define success in a narrow and overly transactional manner.

When the Internet first became a viable marketing medium, marketers measured the success of our websites and online campaigns simply based on the number of hits or impressions we received. But we all know that the number of times an advertisement is seen is not a good indicator of how well a campaign is working. It really is just a decent measurement of how thoroughly an advertising agency spent an intended budget. This metric falls far short of determining how effective a website or an advertisement is because it does not provide any insight into whether a particular hit or impression resulted in a meaningful action.

Online, the majority of marketers have moved beyond measuring hits and impressions to measuring unique visitors and clicks. Now we can tell how many people are visiting which pages of content, how long they spend there, and the path they take to navigate through a site. However, just like hits and impressions, these measurements provide little insight into what actually motivated the person's behavior. Even other metrics like "time on site" or "average page views" provide limited insight about the person and his or her intent and level of active interest. One of my favorite quotes is from Albert Einstein, who says it well: "Not everything that can be counted counts, and not everything that counts can be counted."

I agree that each of these metrics does provide some valuable information, however, they all focus on a single action, usually, the last action a user took. This singular focus on improving only the advertisement that leads to a conversion is often referred to as the "Last Ad" trap.

The Last Ad Trap

In the Last Ad trap, marketers attribute a customer's successful completion of an action solely to a single touch point before the action occurred. For example, a consumer will often click on a banner ad, go to a website, and then make a purchase. The trap that marketers can easily fall into is attributing 100 percent of that conversion to the last ad clicked, thus investing a significant portion of their budget to optimize that one ad — a narrow and solely transactional definition of success.

The problem with this approach is that it does not account for anything the user did *before* he or she clicked on the ad. It does not consider that the user may have visited the company's website before, heard about the company through blogs, received emails from friends about the product, and so on. Instead of considering the holistic impact of the customer's exposure to the brand, the Last Ad trap only considers the effectiveness of a single marketing touch point.

Of course, optimizing ads so that more people are motivated to take action still plays an important role within the larger context of a campaign. However, focusing only on a single ad that delivers the highest conversion rate is like planning a battle and only focusing on the bayonet thrust. It's important, but when planning a campaign for your product you need a more comprehensive, overarching strategy — a strategy that delivers a cohesive experience. Otherwise, the Last Ad trap simply creates an ever-increasing number of disjointed, fragmented campaigns that fail to connect with the more holistic worldview boomers are adopting as they age. (I'll talk more about this concept in Section 3.)

Remember, boomers will often visit a website and fill out an online form, but they are just as likely to get the phone number from the website and call a company's office. Boomers will often read a blog, but won't necessarily post a comment. And boomers often participate in word of mouth by forwarding an email to a friend, after they've read it themselves. However, if you only track the form submission, the comments, or the email open rate, you are not gauging the true effectiveness of your efforts. How then do you reflect the cumulative effect of the multitude of consumer touch points when planning your marketing campaigns?

At Immersion Active, we use a more boomer-friendly measurement of advertising effectiveness — a measurement we call *Meaningful Online Engagement.* For us, Meaningful Online Engagement is a way to measure the effectiveness and value of the sum of all marketing efforts. It means not only considering how many visitors, how many pages they click on, how much time they spend on those pages, and what actions they take, it also means identifying how invested a person is with regard to a specific topic at a particular point in time. Instead of being a single factor that you can measure and monitor, it is a combination of a variety of activities and factors that determine an overall level of intensity.

This intensity is topic-specific and focused on meeting a specific *basic human need*. Once you know how consumers are engaging in this regard, you can then focus your campaign on inserting your brand into these engagements (like a character in a play) with the intent of inspiring the influencers.

In Section 3 of this book, we'll delve into Immersion Active's definition of online engagement specific to baby boomers, which expands on the DRM approach, to provide insight into how the sum of consumer engagements can be monitored and measured.

Establishing a Framework for Replicable Success

So, even if you gain an understanding of the basic needs driving human behavior and you take a more holistic, engagement-based approach to creating and measuring your marketing campaigns, how can you deliver successful marketing campaigns over and over again?

We've occasionally heard successful marketing described as "a crap shoot," but we recently heard a better gambling analogy: Today, campaign planning is a bit like playing a slot machine. If you can get the perfect alignment of creative development, media planning, and interactive implementation (i.e., all your cherries line up), you hit the jackpot. Otherwise, you have to keep dropping your money in and pulling the lever, hoping to hit the right combination. In other words, you're counting on luck.

Too often, marketers do not approach campaigns with a framework that considers the efficient integration of the creative, the media through which it will be delivered, and the interactive technology used to deliver it. Instead, the creative is often developed by one department, which then sends it to another department (or another agency entirely) to handle the media. Yet again, someone else determines how that creative is going to be delivered via which technology.

Often, technology can negatively impact the creative, and vice versa. How many times have you heard someone in your technical department say, "We can't do that because…"? Or, because certain technologies, such as blogs, social networks, or widgets, are hot, the campaign is developed around those technologies without aligning them with the overall strategy. As Steve Jobs once said, "Design is not just what it looks and feels like. Design is how it works." (That will be my one Steve Jobs reference, I promise.)

Although it is often the case, the problem isn't only that distinct departments are not working together. The larger issue is that many marketers are faced with a disparate group of skill sets that have no process for working in harmony. Generally, creative development, media planning, and interactive considerations do not come together seamlessly, as they should for cohesive campaigns.

And even when a campaign *is* successful, marketers can rarely provide a definitive conclusion as to why it succeeded, thus significantly decreasing their chances of replicating that success in the next campaign.

To address this problem, we've created a model based on our Meaningful Online Engagement definition — a strategic planning framework that merges creative, media, and interactive elements into an integrated approach to engaging boomers online. It is the combination of three strategies, each of which build off of the other, that enables you to create campaigns that encompass a thematic online experience for your brand. (Otherwise it's just a gamble.)

The Take-Away

To successfully appeal to baby boomers, marketers need to have a deeper understanding of human behavior, a more holistic measurement of marketing effectiveness, and a framework for replicating success. In short, DRM and Meaningful Online Engagement offer the solution to these problems and make it possible to more effectively connect with boomer consumers in today's aging, yet vital society.

Section 2:
Motivating Boomers Online

In Section 1 we covered the size of the boomer market and the potential of the Internet to reach this influential consumer group. But, more important, we talked about the inherent flaws in today's marketing approaches — flaws that make current marketing practices ineffective and make marketers' jobs even more difficult.

To overcome these challenges, we need to shift to a new marketing paradigm, away from product-centric messages and toward consumer-centric messages. This paradigm shift begins by gaining a deeper understanding of what motivates consumers, especially boomer consumers, to take action. It completes by employing a new approach to engaging your audience in conversations about your brand.

We'll talk more about engagement in Section 3, but first, it's important to understand what motivates consumers to take action, whether that action is buying products, submitting a contact form, participating in a blog, or interacting with a video.

Chapter 3:
The Biology of Marketing

"If they say why, why? Tell 'em that it's human nature."

— Michael Jackson, *"Human Nature"*

The underlying philosophy that is the key to not only this book but to every project Immersion Active undertakes is Developmental Relationship Marketing (DRM). DRM is a marketing approach based on the premise that a person's developmental maturity and season of life predispose their worldviews and needs; how they go about meeting those needs; and how their brain processes information. The beauty of DRM is that it facilitates a more complete, holistic view of consumers, through which marketers can understand the underlying motivators of human behavior.

When trying to understand DRM, it's important to start by understanding some basic biological principles on how humans think and process information. Volumes of textbooks have been written on the human mind — I can't possibly convey all of that information to you within a single chapter. Instead, I'll focus on five key concepts:

- The definition of behavior
- The biology of behavior

- The conscious and unconscious brain
- Lead with the right, follow with the left
- Emotions and feelings

The Definition of Behavior

According to Dictionary.com (I couldn't resist), behavior is defined as an "observable activity in a human or animal; the aggregate of responses to internal and external stimuli; and a stereotyped, species-specific activity."

In other words, behavior is doing something. It's taking an action. All marketers know that the goal of marketing is to *get large numbers of people to take a specific, desired action.* That's the sum of it. As marketers, we want to influence consumer behavior, whether we like to think of it that way or not.

However, in order to influence behavior, it's necessary to understand what it is about people that makes them act the way they do. It may sound simple: When we're hungry, we eat, when we're tired, we sleep. But the intricacies of human behavior go way beyond satisfying basic physical needs. Scholars, scientists, philosophers, and politicians have spent lifetimes trying to figure out human behavior — and I certainly would not suggest that this book has unlocked these secrets.

Luckily, in order to market effectively to the masses, you don't have to understand all human behaviors — you only need to understand the basic, *common* behaviors that all humans share, regardless of age, sex, income, or ethnicity. By understanding these *shared* behaviors, you can then develop marketing messages that connect with them on a broader and deeper level, thus connecting with the largest possible target audience, without worrying about the subtle distinctions traditional segmentation models often suffer from.

The Biology of Behavior

Maybe a more appropriate way to introduce this chapter would have been through the lyrics of Sam Cooke: "Don't know much about history. Don't know much about biology. Don't know much about a science book…" You get the drift. I'm not trying to turn marketers into scientists and I do not believe marketing is a science. But, I do believe that the best way to learn about basic human behaviors is to understand the biology of behavior.

At its most basic level, our biological makeup is defined by our DNA, which is the biochemical encoder of humans. At the DNA level, any two humans are 99.9 percent the same. So, a large portion of human behavior is going to be similar. Regardless of age, sex, economic status, or any other factor, human beings often act in a similar manner given a certain situation. Additionally, not only do humans of the 21st century age, mature, and grow in a similar fashion, humans throughout modern history generally behaved in similar ways. By nature, our DNA biases our behavior toward perpetuation of humankind as a species. In other words, all humans are biologically driven to not only survive, but to succeed and to thrive.

People often think that we stop growing once we reach adulthood, but that's a bit shortsighted. We continuously grow from the time we take our first breath until we take our last. Physically, we may not get any taller after we reach our mid-twenties, but our mental processes, our behavioral tendencies, and even the way our brains are wired constantly change as we age. DNA predefines just as much of our non-physical growth as it predefines our facial features, height, or the fact that we walk upright.

And during each period of growth, humans will *generally* behave similarly because we are trying to fulfill similar biological needs: Children learn the rules of society in order to survive; young adults partake in courting rituals to find a mate; older adults pass down their history and lessons learned to help ensure the success of the next generation. Where an individual is within nature's pre-defined growth stages can be referred to as an individual's *personal maturation level.* And this maturation level will generally determine his or her needs, values, worldviews, and cognitive style. In other words, someone's level of personal development can be used to help predict behavior. This concept is the biology of behavior.

Let's be realistic though. If all human behavior was dictated by our biological makeup, we would all act the same and marketing would be a breeze. However, there are two sides to all human behavior: the biological (where we are all the same) and the psychological (where we are all different). In a sense, we are all made up of the same stuff (DNA), but we are all different — a concept that evokes the age-old "nature versus nurture" debate. While we are genetically more than 99 percent the same, there are a number of psychological factors that also affect how people behave — everyone is unique.

What's crucial to understanding behavior, and thus the effectiveness of marketing, is to *grasp how our biological similarities interact with our psychological differences.* Biology initiates, but psychology disposes, as my friend and mentor David Wolfe says. In other words, psychological differences dictate how we consciously control our biologically driven behavior. But how?

The Conscious and Unconscious Brain

Contemporary brain research has found that 95 percent of the mental activity that goes on in our brain is performed outside of our conscious mind.[42] Our brains are bombarded with a myriad of sensory inputs every second, including everything going on both inside and outside of our bodies simultaneously. It is simply impossible for our conscious minds to process all of this information on a conscious level, which is why much of it is performed in our unconscious brain.

When we receive information, our unconscious brain first determines if the information is important enough to pass on to our conscious minds for further evaluation. This filtering and prioritizing of information is what David Wolfe refers to as "information triage."

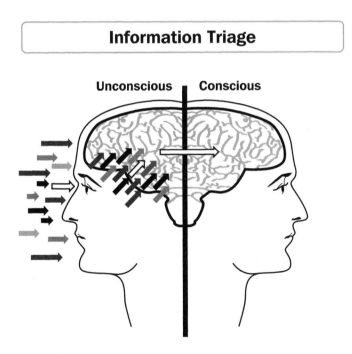

Here's a good example of information triage: Imagine that you are at a party, deeply engaged in conversation. Suddenly, you hear your name in another conversation across the room and you stop to listen.

Although you may think that you are just beginning to listen to that conversation, your unconscious brain was hearing the conversation the entire time. However, it wasn't until your name came up that your unconscious brain decided to make your conscious mind aware of it.

Therefore, in order for the conscious brain to be aware of something, it must first survive the information triage of the unconscious brain. So, then, one of the primary rules of DRM (or of any effective marketing approach) must be to determine how to survive information triage and gain "permission" into the consciousness of the consumer — to obtain landing rights. And a key to obtaining landing rights is to make an emotional connection with the consumer by "leading with the right and following with the left."

Lead with the Right; Follow with the Left

I'm not trying to turn marketers into Rocky. (OK, maybe I am.) But the theory is the same for marketing messages as it is for boxers: Get the person's attention with the initial contact and then solidify your position (or knock 'em out) with the follow-up. From a brain-science perspective, that means connecting with the more emotional nature of the right side of the brain and then following with more factual, left-brain information.

In general, marketers have only about two-tenths to eight-tenths of a second to gain landing rights in the conscious mind. In other words, it only takes a fraction of a second for our unconscious brains to determine what is important enough to make us consciously aware of it. So how do you make that connection in such a short time period and with enough impact for the unconscious mind to pay attention? The key is emotion.

Too often I talk to marketers who are obsessed with the benefits, features, and options their products offer. Sure, these features are important aspects of the product, but research has shown that if marketing messages only provide consumers with facts and figures, the message will not connect with consumer (especially older consumers) on the same level as a message that invokes their emotions — even at the expense of providing less information.

In fact, a recent study by The Boomer Project showed that, when given comparable advertisements (shown below), consumers felt that the advertisement that connected with them emotionally was more informative than the advertisement that did not, even though each ad contained the same amount of factual information.

The more emotional ad (B) was preferred 3-to-1 and perceived as more informative.

Ideally, all brands should be processed emotionally before they are processed rationally. Additionally, research has shown that if you make an emotional connection with an older consumer first, they will not only absorb the logistical information later, but they will generally consume *more* information than their younger counterparts.

If you lead with the facts instead of emotions, consumers may hear your arguments, but you won't gain the same landing rights you would have if you had made an initial emotional connection. Remember: unconscious to conscious *or* right to left.

Emotions and Conscious Decisions

Emotions are physical responses initiated in our brain when it connects an external stimulus with internal information we already possess. This physical basis for emotion is important: Emotions typically elicit some physiological response from within our bodies. The unconscious brain determines the strength of these responses by the amount of relevance it places on the stimulus. It then determines what information to pass on to the conscious brain and with what priority. Once the information has reached your conscious brain, many physiological factors can then come into play as your body determines its actual response.

The amount of conscious control we have over our emotions and the relationship between emotions and decisions is often heatedly debated among psychologists, sociologists, and researchers. For us, as marketers, however, the important thing to remember is that emotions are what make information relevant to the consumer. They are "the glue that holds together all voluntary relationships, whether they are relationships with other people or with companies and brands[43]."

Emotional connections are even more crucial when marketing to older consumers because older consumers are more likely to follow "their gut reaction." As we age, we make increasing use of intuition. We put trust in first impressions, which are emotionally generated, and generally trust our feelings more[44]. If you want your marketing messages to get landing rights and survive information triage, you need to make an emotional connection with your target consumers. (Chapter 6 will provide more guidance on making this emotional connection.)

Kleenex's Emotional Connection

"Have you ever laughed until you cried? Had a tear-filled hello or goodbye?" In a recent multichannel marketing campaign, titled "Let It Out," Kleenex® brand asks real-life consumers to share what gets them a little choked up. And more importantly, it shows that when those tears start to flow, Kleenex tissues will be there.

For this campaign, Kleenex released a series of television commercials that featured man-on-the-street encounters with real people in metropolitan settings. Prompted with very few questions, these everyday people delve into personal issues, such as the death of a loved one and relationship troubles, ending with the subjects (and probably many of the viewers themselves) in tears.

The online component is an entire "Let It Out" section on the brand's website. An intro video, featuring snippets from many of the different commercials, delicately introduces users to the campaign, primarily through close ups on people dabbing their eyes with tissues, wiping their noses on their sleeves, and apologizing for letting their emotions take over. Accompanying text reads, "It's time to LAUGH until you CRY. SCREAM until you spit. Show your LOVE and show some tears. SING at the top of your lungs. Jump for JOY. And when tons of STUFF stuffs up your nose, BLOW it loud and blow it proud. It's time to let it out."

From there, users can explore other people's stories and "Experience the Release." The site gently eases users into the experience by encouraging them to "see how others have let it out" in eight categories: Laugh, Cry, Love, Sing, Joy, Stuff, Blow, Scream. As they are browsing, users can click on a Kleenex tissue box icon to give a tissue to a user whose story moved them. And if a user feels moved to share his or her own story, Kleenex reassuringly asks, "Are you ready? Go ahead and let it out. You'll feel a lot better."

This user-centric experience shows that it's OK to cry every once and a while. It creates an emotional connection with consumers and the Kleenex brand by assuring consumers that emotions are nothing to be ashamed of, exemplified by the real people featured in the television commercials and on the website. In the intro video, a line concludes, "Turns out, all it takes is a good listener and Kleenex tissues." With this campaign, it looks like Kleenex became both.

 Read more online at
www.dotboombook.com/kleenex

The Take-Away

So now you can see that one of the tenants of DRM is that our biology and our DNA significantly influence most human behaviors. In addition:

- Nature predefines many similar behaviors across all generations.

- Our behavior is influenced by how we actually process information. The unconscious brain performs information triage on the information we take in to determine what is important enough to gain "landing rights" in the conscious brain.

- The best way to survive information triage is to make an emotional connection through our right brain. Emotions are physical responses and the strength of those responses is directly related to the level of relevance the unconscious brain gives the information.

- As consumers age, they are generally more influenced by their initial, emotional reactions.

Chapter 4:
The Psychology of Boomer Minds

"Now you have class. Now you have splash. Now you have mass motivation."

— David Bowie, *"That's Motivation"*

The key to any effective marketing approach is to survive information triage and make it into a consumer's consciousness. Then you can effectively show how your brand can meet that consumer's basic needs, which are what motivates them to take action. But how do you know what those basic needs are?

Many noted philosophers, psychologists, and marketers have put forth numerous (and often complex) definitions of the most basic human needs. Don't worry; you don't need to learn them all. After much examination and scrutiny, Jonathan and I determined two that we feel are most relevant to mature marketing: David Wolfe's core values and Abraham Maslow's Hierarchy of Needs.

Wolfe's Core Values

David Wolfe, author of *Ageless Marketing* and *Firms of Endearment*, proposes that all behavior is motivated by the psychological need to fulfill five core values. It is the need to meet these five core values that motivates all human behavior. These core values include:

- *Identity values*

- *Relationship values*

- *Purpose values*

- *Adaptation values*

- *Energy values*

Identity Values

Identity values revolve around self-preservation, self-awareness, and self-image. Notice a trend here? It is all about the self. Identity values are needs that, when fulfilled, allow you to become who you are. They are the primary motivators behind human achievement. Yet despite being so focused on self, Identity values tend to be outwardly focused in the first half of life. Younger people feel as though they are constantly judged by their peers, and therefore project themselves as they would like others to see them. I have seen this firsthand as my son, Gabe, enters his teenage years. Now, it's all about what other kids will think, how other kids will react, and worst of all, if the girls will notice!

However, as a person moves into the second half of life, his or her Identity values become more inwardly focused. As people age, their social circles become narrower and people begin to care less about others' judgments of them. Remember our boomers Robert and Mary? Frankly, Robert wastes little energy worrying about what other people think about him — instead he prefers to focus his energy on activities that make him feel fulfilled. And Mary has started reading more, expressing her desire to learn more about the world around her.

The Values at a Glance[45]

Identity values involve self-preservation, self-awareness, and self-image.

Relationship values involve connections to others, institutions, and beliefs.

Purpose values involve meaning and validation of one's life and actions.

Adaptation values involve the skills and knowledge necessary to negotiate life.

Energy values involve health, well-being, and functionality.

Older adults tend to focus more on servicing the inner self, truly becoming the person they have spent countless years defining. Furthermore, Identity values drive us to recreate ourselves in everything we do. For consumers in the second half of life, the identity they spent years establishing will live on through their legacy. That's why wealthy benefactors set up foundations, leave money to worthy causes…you get the idea.

Therefore, when trying to fulfill their Identity values, consumers want brands to show them how the brand can reflect who they are or who they want to be. They want to know how the brand can help achieve a more idealized version of themselves and push them to be most successful.

The best example of the difference between the way older and younger adults fulfill their Identity needs came from one of Jonathan's and my employees, who is 46. When asked what she likes about her sporty little Mercedes Benz convertible (which was a gift from her husband), she said: "It's relaxing. When I've had a stressful day, I just hop in the car, put the top down, turn up my '70s music, and drive. I love feeling the wind in my hair and the sun on my face, both of which whisk my problems away. It just feels luxurious. Sure, I get lots of compliments on the car, especially from younger guys who think it's really hot. But for me, I hardly even notice what it looks like. It's just the way it makes me feel." While it may seem unbelievable that someone does not care about the appearance of a car as nice as this one, I've known her for quite some time — and I believe her reflection and sentiment to be true.

Relationship Values

It's not difficult to determine what's at the heart of this core value: relationships. People need companionship and interaction with others to feel happy and healthy. However, Relationship values are not limited to connections with others. They also encompass relationships with beliefs, institutions, and organizations that guide people through their everyday lives.

As with all of Wolfe's values, Relationship values shift as a person moves into the second half of their life. Younger people value relationships for what they can gain from them, whether it be finding a romantic partner or scoring a promotion — all with a focus on their social lives. However, older adults are generally more concerned with what they put into a relationship than what they get out of it. They seek comfort and pleasure in stable relationships in which they can both give and receive.

As we described in Chapter 1, family is extremely important to Carol. Her Relationship values drive many of her consumer decisions. Consider that in the past two years, Carol and her husband have taken the entire family on two Disney cruises (that's a total of 17 people on each cruise) and paid for everyone's trip. Why? Carol wanted to experience Disney with all of her family in one place at one time. Or consider that even when she can barely get out of bed, Carol will travel two hours to watch her grandson play football or go to the church picnic at the local park. For Carol, relationships are at her core and brands that help her fulfill her Relationship values will most successfully connect with her.

Perhaps one of the best examples of marketing messages that conveys a brand's ability to meet Relationship values can be seen in the Coca-Cola commercial featuring one person handing another a Coke. We all know the tagline — "Have a Coke and a smile." Whether the bottle passes from a grandfather to granddaughter, a sophisticated woman to a sweaty construction worker, or a polar bear to a penguin, the message is the same: Coke helps you connect with other people to form more meaningful relationships. And it works. The simple fact that almost everyone, regardless of their age, can recall at least one example of a Coke commercial shows how effective these messages are.

It's even surprising how much I've taken that emotional connection to Coke to heart. My first job out of college was at a small graphics service bureau. I can remember when we were on a tight deadline or things were a little stressful, I would offer to run across the street and buy everyone a "Happy Coke." Back then, I didn't realize why it was Coke I was buying. (I actually prefer Pepsi.) But regardless of the situation, a "Happy Coke" never failed to break the tension.

Living the Brand

It's important to note here that a company's *professed* persona and *perceived* persona are often vastly different. In other words, the marketing messages companies put forth may vary greatly from how their consumers actually view their brand. Companies whose professed and perceived personas do not match are at serious risk. However, the situation is even more threatening if you are trying to leverage that persona to connect with a consumer and show them how that brand can meet their Relationship needs.

Rather, marketing messages that appeal to a person's Relationship values need to facilitate a relationship between the consumer and the product or brand. Corporate personas need to be congruent in the marketplace and within the company. "Having a great tagline does not a great brand make," Wolfe states in *Ageless Marketing*. "However, taglines often indicate something about a company's corporate persona — its public face. Ideally...a company's real self and its social self are in harmony. It's called 'living the brand[46].'"

Take a look, for example, at Kashi foods, which has a tag line of "7 whole grains on a mission." Its website is all about providing a place where people can not only find information about Kashi products, but, more important, find and share information about healthier living, even going as far to sponsor a "Day of Change" event. The company provides tools to help people make healthier choices, not just purchase its products. These tools show Kashi's investment in bettering the lives of its consumers, thus establishing a relationship with them to live happier and healthier lives.

Read more online at
www.dotboombook.com/kashi

Purpose Values

Throughout human history, countless philosophers, theologians, scientists, pundits, and average Joes have searched for the meaning of life. Purpose values encompass this search and extend beyond meaning to a desire for validation of one's life and actions. Every living organism, not just humans, needs to have a purpose in order to survive. In fact, I was amazed to learn that the drive for a purposeful existence is so strong that, if a cell no longer has a function in the human body, it will self-destruct. Without a purpose, the cell has no reason to exist.

Purpose values can be the strongest motivators in human behavior, yet as Wolfe points out, they receive the least attention in marketing communication[47].

It is not uncommon for aging adults to feel a decrease in purpose. Retirement, especially among men, and empty nests, especially among women, often leave older adults feeling unfulfilled. Often, these adults will turn to community service and charities as a way to fulfill their Purpose needs. Consider Robert's drive to still head the booster club, coach lacrosse, and run the concession stand. Giving back to the community, volunteering, and maintaining a sense of social consciousness help boomers and seniors meet their Purpose needs (among others).

Traditional nonprofit organizations have always been rooted in Purpose values, looking to fulfill a consumer's drive for purpose through altruistic means. The Susan G. Komen for the Cure Foundation is the world's largest and most progressive grassroots network for breast cancer survivors and activists. For its nationwide "Race for the Cure" series of 5K races, the foundation created a website where registrants can personalize their own Web page to encourage and solicit fundraising for the race. Registrants can add personal stories, upload their own photographs, incorporate widgets to display fundraising goals, and much more — all a direct reflection of their purpose-driven values to raise the most amount of money they can for the cause.

Adaptation Values

Living in a modern society does not obliterate the need to develop the skills and knowledge necessary to negotiate life. Most people can easily identify Adaptation values early in life. As my children grew from infants to young adults, I watched them play and go to school to learn the life skills they need to survive. Often (sometimes too often), this play involved novelty, experimentation, and thrill-seeking (or hair-raising) behaviors that helped them explore and expand their universe.

Despite popular belief, however, Adaptation values do not diminish when we graduate from high school. Throughout our lives, we continually need to learn new skills to adapt to our life situations, whether we are getting married, having a child, or taking on a new job. And as we continue to age, our need to adapt becomes even more significant as we face challenges of retirement, having grandchildren, caring for aging parents, declining health, and more. Imagine the Adaptation needs Mary is trying to fulfill as she adjusts to her daughter moving back in, her father's potential need for care, and her husband's prospective job change.

Boomers are currently facing more simultaneously occurring life events than other consumer groups. Thus, boomers have more Adaptation needs than any other generation. And what's especially unique about boomers is that they are going about coping with their overlapping life events in a less predictable manner than generations before.

Showing baby boomers how you can help meet these Adaptation values is a strong behavioral motivator. Having the skills to cope with whatever we face not only impacts our Adaptation values, but also has a significant impact on our Purpose, Relationship, Identity, and Energy values as well.

An example of a brand that helps baby boomers meet their Adaptation values is Home Instead Senior Care, a client of our company, Immersion Active. Home Instead offers non-medical, in-home care for seniors. Their services provide busy adult children, like Mary, with skilled, professional help to care for their aging parents. Home Instead Senior Care's marketing efforts help fulfill boomers' Adaptation needs by providing free online and print resources, a website where family caregivers can take a stress assessment, and online videos showing how to talk to aging parents about sensitive topics.

Energy Values

Energy needs generate behaviors that promote physical and psychological health and enhance functional performance and well being. They also motivate people's desire for a change of pace and play the lead role in a drive for a fit and healthy lifestyle. Energy values "lie behind much of our behavior that is oriented to the pursuit of sensuous pleasures, without which, well, life would hardly be worth living[48]."

Younger people often fulfill Energy values through adventurous activities that break their daily routines — a way of "recharging their batteries." In the second half of life, people's Energy values become tamer, but they do not disappear. Rather, these needs may be met by more leisurely (but still productive) pursuits such as gardening, volunteer work, hiking, crafts, and hobbies.

Wolfe points out that there is also a key psychological distinction between early-life Energy values and later-life Energy values: self-indulgence versus self-expression. The former is hedonistic, while the latter is existential. Have you ever heard the phrase, "stop and smell the roses?" Chances are that advice came from an older adult, to a younger adult, encouraging them to slow down and enjoy life's subtleties.

An older mind can extract pleasure from even the smallest stimuli, often leading to more "peak experiences" (as we'll discuss shortly). Therefore, messaging and imagery that evoke the five senses can be especially effective with mature minds because they allow an older consumer to insert him or herself into a sensual experience, appealing to their subtler, but often more appreciated, Energy values. To meet her Energy needs, Carol has taken up crocheting and knitting. Robert likes to browse the Web for the latest lacrosse highlights and coaching tips. And when Mary has a moment to recharge, she likes to simply take a walk around her neighborhood at sunset.

One of the best examples of a brand appealing to Energy values is, as you may (or may not) expect, the erectile dysfunction medication Cialis. Beyond the obvious sexual Energy value this product fulfills, Cialis' marketing messages tap into our senses to make an emotional connection: partners subtly caress each other (touch), share a romantic dinner (taste), offer flowers (smell), listen to nostalgic or romantic music (sound), and share secret smiles (sight). All these messages unconsciously and sensuously connect with our emotions and show how Cialis can fulfill many Energy values.

It's All Relative

As shown in our discussion of Adaptation values, all of Wolfe's core values are interrelated. Just as the primary colors blend to make all of the colors of the rainbow, a combination of core values underlies all human behavior. Note how, in our discussion above, Robert, Carol, and Mary generally experienced all of the core values. These values are all present in all humans all of the time, but in varying shades of priority.

If Mary's Relationship needs are being met (which they may be with three children living at home), she may be more focused on her Energy needs. That doesn't mean that her relationships aren't important to her, and in fact, they would probably become a priority if threatened, but at this point in time, she has a greater *unfulfilled* need for energy.

The key, then, for successfully marketing to Mary and any other boomer, is to understand which needs your brand can help fulfill and then to craft your marketing strategies and tactics to connect with consumers who are focused on fulfilling those needs. (We'll discuss this in greater detail in Section 3.)

Maslow's Hierarchy of Needs

In addition to Wolfe's core values, a second definition of human needs plays an important role in determining mature consumers' behavior. Abraham Maslow, who is widely considered to be the father of humanistic psychology, developed the pyramid-shaped Hierarchy of Needs. His hierarchy is based on the premise that our biological needs are hierarchical and that you cannot truly meet higher level needs until the lower level needs have been adequately fulfilled.

**Abraham Maslow's
Hierarchy of Needs**

Self-Actualization

Esteem

Love & Belonging

Safety & Security

Basic Physiological

Maslow has divided his hierarchy into five levels of needs: physiological, safety and security, love and belonging, esteem, and self-actualization. According to Maslow, these levels identify the primary needs a person is trying to fulfill within their lives. Fulfilling the needs at one level of the hierarchy will be a person's primary focus until those needs are met. Only after the majority of those needs are met will the person begin to focus on the next higher level of needs. Where a person is within Maslow's hierarchy is called their *developmental maturation level.*

Throughout our lives, we are constantly striving to move toward higher level needs and, according to Maslow, this desire to reach higher levels of developmental maturation is biologically driven. We cannot consciously decide that we want to move up or down within the pyramid, but instead are naturally driven to fulfill higher level needs as our lower level needs are met.

The Needs at a Glance

Physiological needs: A person's physiological needs include the basic needs for survival, such as air, water, food, warmth, and shelter.

Safety needs: The yearning for protection, security, order, and stability are encompassed by our safety needs. Maslow also includes religious beliefs as a safety need because such beliefs provide a way of organizing the universe in a coherent and secure manner.

Love and belonging needs: Whether it be intimate social connections, like family members, sexual partners, and friendships, or larger group settings, like workplaces, religious groups, and recreational organizations, human beings need to belong and to feel loved. Maslow emphasizes that love is not synonymous with sex. In fact, many study sexual activity as a physiological need.

Esteem needs: All humans have an innate desire for self respect as well as to be respected by others. This desire includes various kinds of achievement, status, responsibility, and reputation. Esteem needs have two aspects: first, the desire for strength, achievement, adequacy, independence, freedom, and confidence from within, and; second is the desire for prestige, recognition, attention, importance, or appreciation from other people. Older adults more often strive for the first type of esteem, which focuses more on self, whereas younger adults more often strive for recognition and attention from their peers.

Self-actualization needs: Kurt Goldstein, a German neurologist and psychiatrist, originally coined the phrase *self-actualization* to mean the desire to become more of what one is and to become everything that a person is capable of being. Maslow interpreted self-actualization as an advanced state of psychological maturity where people are truly enlightened. The specific nature of self-actualization will vary greatly from person to person. But in general, this is a state where people feel more individual, spiritual, altruistic, autonomous, realistic, and authentic.

Moving Up and Down within the Hierarchy

At the same time, a person's level of developmental maturation is not always an upward progression. If, for any reason, a person's lower level needs are no longer being met, then they will move down the pyramid until those lower level needs are fulfilled once again. Consider Carol, who after 30 years of marriage, divorced. While Carol may have been striving to fulfill her esteem needs prior to her divorce, afterwards, she progressed down the pyramid to focus on her love and belonging needs.

It is also important to note that the needs on one level do not need to be completely satisfied before a person begins to strive for the next level. While our needs may be focused on love and belonging at a particular point in life, we will begin to seek fulfillment of our esteem needs as well. Once Carol had moved beyond her divorce, she started to seek out new activities and adventures, such as organizing a family vacation, which helped her feel good about herself.

Given the hierarchical nature of Maslow's pyramid and the fact that we continually strive to reach higher levels of developmental maturation, you may assume that older adults are more likely to be self-actualized. While it is true that older adults are generally striving to fulfill their esteem and self-actualizing needs, Maslow estimated that only two percent of the population ever becomes truly self-actualized.

Most Likely to Succeed

Note that while a person's developmental maturation level cannot simply be determined by their age, financial status, or education background, there does seem to be some correlation between socio-economic status and maturation level. The more educated and affluent a consumer, the more likely they are to be seeking fulfillment of their higher level needs. These characteristics correspond well with the older consumers who are more likely to be online.

What's most important to recognize is that everyone, from the youngest infant to the oldest adult, experiences self actualizing moments, or *peak experiences*, throughout our lives. Think about a baby's first coo. That's a peak experience for both the baby and his parents (their first moment of communication). Or, I think about my grandfather who loved to take me camping. Sharing that perfect sunrise over the Appalachian Mountains with his grandson provided him with a peak experience he and I talked about for years.

Peak experiences give us glimpses of what it would be like to be a self-actualized individual. Even when we are struggling to meet our most basic needs, we strive for peak experiences. But when marketing to boomers and seniors, it's especially important to recognize the importance of peak experiences, because the desire to experience them, as well as the number and intensity of those experiences, tends to increase with age. So our task, as marketers, becomes to associate our brand with those peak experiences, either through the marketing messages we deliver or through the products themselves.

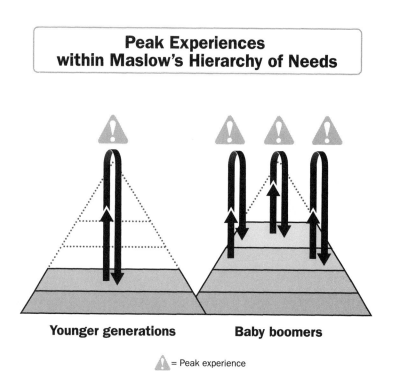

Peak Experiences within Maslow's Hierarchy of Needs

Younger generations   Baby boomers

⚠ = Peak experience

That association with peak experiences makes it important to understand where your target consumers lie within the hierarchy. If a brand's target consumer group is focused on fulfilling their esteem needs, but the marketing strategy and messaging is targeted on love and belonging, the marketing efforts probably will not be as effective. Also, remember that individuals in one level of the hierarchy are always striving to move up to the next level and that people have peak experiences within all levels of the hierarchy. If your strategy includes showing how your brand can offer self-actualizing, or peak, experiences for a person regardless of their current level, your messages will resonate much more effectively.

The Take-Away

This chapter covered two deeply rooted psychological systems that define basic human needs. And it is the inevitable drive to meet these needs that motivates human behavior.

- Wolfe's core values consist of Identity, Relationship, Purpose, Adaptation, and Energy values. While these values are present in everyone, how we go about meeting those needs, and which are of primary importance, changes as a person ages.

- Maslow's Hierarchy of Needs consists of five levels: physiological, safety and security, love and belonging, esteem, and self-actualization. These needs are arranged in a pyramid form and throughout our lives, we strive to move up the pyramid once lower level needs are met.

- Regardless of where an individual is within Maslow's Hierarchy, we all strive for peak experiences that give us a glimpse of what a truly self-actualized person might be.

- The combination of Wolfe's core values and Maslow's Hierarchy of Needs provide us with significant insight into what motivates boomer consumer behavior.

Chapter 5:
A Shift in Boomer Thinking

"To everything – turn, turn, turn. There is a season – turn, turn, turn"

— The Byrds, *"Turn! Turn! Turn!"*

Before I move forward, let's take a minute to review what's been covered thus far about DRM and motivating baby boomers. First and foremost, motivating boomers relies on understanding that human behavior is heavily influenced by our biological makeup. Our DNA predisposes our behaviors and our unconscious brain plays a significant role in determining what information is passed on to our conscious mind. Emotions, in particular, play an important role in gaining landing rights and surviving information triage in the unconscious brain.

Psychologically, all humans are on a quest to fulfill certain core needs that we all share. Meeting these needs, as defined by both Wolfe and Maslow, is something we are unconsciously and continuously trying to accomplish. And aligning your brand with the fulfillment of these needs is a successful way to connect with boomer consumers.

So now what?

To Divide or Unite

Traditional marketing philosophies have always assumed that you need to divide the universe of potential consumers into segments to target them most effectively. Consumer segmentation is often based on factors such as age, race, economic status, and education level. And when it comes to segmenting boomers, there are almost as many segmentation models as there are boomers.

Segmentation, by definition, means to break something into smaller groups or pieces, so it makes sense that boundaries for those groups are needed. However, this type of segmentation is exclusionary because it is determined by differences. By segmenting the universe of potential customers in this manner, you are narrowing your potential audience.

DRM, on the other hand, takes a different approach. When you focus your marketing efforts on connecting with consumers' needs, you are casting a wider net, inviting more consumers to connect with your brand. By addressing common human characteristics, DRM is inclusionary rather than exclusionary.

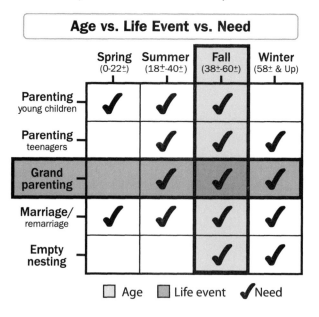

	Spring (0-22±)	Summer (18±-40±)	Fall (38±-60±)	Winter (58± & Up)
Parenting young children	✓	✓	✓	
Parenting teenagers		✓	✓	✓
Grand parenting		✓	✓	✓
Marriage/ remarriage	✓	✓	✓	✓
Empty nesting			✓	✓

☐ Age ◼ Life event ✓ Need

So, how do you connect your brand with these common human characteristics? How do you determine which ads to create, where to place them, and what they should say? How do you engage your consumer and move them to take a specific action? In Section 3 of *Dot Boom*, we'll provide you with a framework for answering these specific questions. For now, the important thing to remember is that you need to focus on including people because of their similarities, rather than excluding them because of their differences, when trying to develop the most effective boomer marketing campaigns.

Showing Boomers How You Meet Their Needs

So how do you include the most people in your marketing campaign and how do you connect them with your brand? Start by determining what needs your brand fulfills, and then connect them to consumers' needs.

Take a moment and think about it. Does your brand help consumers fulfill Purpose, Relationship, Identity, Energy, or Adaptation values? How does it appeal to people in different levels of Maslow's hierarchy? Take a minute to go back and review the definitions of these needs in Chapter 4. Chances are your brand will help fulfill multiple values and needs, but for the purposes of a specific campaign or marketing strategy, what are the primary needs you are trying to fulfill? Keep those needs foremost in your mind as you read the rest of *Dot Boom*. Write them down if you need to.

I know that as a marketer, you want to tap into the powerful boomer market. So how do you show boomers the connection between your product and the fulfillment of their needs?

Everyone from the youngest child to the oldest adult has the same core needs, but how they go about fulfilling those needs changes as we grow. You'll probably agree that a 25-year-old views the world very differently than a 15-year-old. Twenty-five-year-olds are often thinking about careers, apartments, marriage, or perhaps starting a family. Fifteen-year-olds are thinking about homework, cleaning their room, and the girl or boy up the street.

However, what many people often fail to recognize is how the views of a 45-year-old differ from those of a 25-year-old or how the views of a 65-year-old differ from those of a 45-year-old. Forty-five-year-olds may be focused on preparing for retirement, first (and often second) mortgages, and staying in touch with their spouse despite the demands of work and family. On the other hand, 65-year-olds may be thinking about volunteering at the hospital, downsizing to a retirement community, and simply walking hand-in-hand with their spouse of 40 years. All of these individuals have Identity, Relationship, Purpose, Energy, and Adaptation needs. They just go about meeting those needs in different ways.

Need Fulfillment by Age

People will see that I'm important

I've worked hard and I deserve this

I'll enjoy the comfort and handling

25-year-old   45-year-old   65-year-old

Fortunately, since basic human growth is pre-defined by our molecular make-up (our DNA), it is possible to draw some predictive conclusions about how a person will strive to fulfill their core needs during a particular time of life, specifically, their season of life.

The Seasons of Life

People's lives are often described as being divided into four seasons: Spring, Summer, Fall, and Winter:

- Spring is usually considered as the period from birth to 22± years old.

- Summer covers anywhere from ages 18± to 40±.

- Fall is generally from age 38± to age 60±.

- Winter is roughly age 58± and up.

During each of these seasons, humans will generally have similar developmental objectives and catalysts that are indicative of how they will fulfill their basic core needs.

Obviously, boomers are entering the Fall and Winter of their lives. As they do so, they undergo a personal paradigm shift wherein they become less outwardly focused and more inwardly focused. Fall in particular is a period where adults begin to strive to maintain a balance between their personal and professional lives, (which I see playing out in my own life), search for meaning in life, and often realize that life didn't work out exactly as expected. In this regard, people in the Fall of their lives, as opposed to those in the Spring or Summer, will try to fulfill their needs in very different ways.

For example, on a recent company retreat, our younger employees (those in the Summer of their lives) decided to go for a run and play basketball to re-energize themselves after a long brainstorming session. Our older employees, those in the Fall, snuggled up with a good book, did crossword puzzles, and took a leisurely walk around the block. They were all fulfilling their Energy needs, but in very different ways.

The seasons of life can loosely be interpreted as a segmentation model, since they can be used to focus marketing efforts and narrow your target audience. However, unlike traditional segmentation models, which generally further segment each season based on smaller age brackets, income, education, gender, ethnicity, or similar demographics, the seasons of life are simply a way for you to better identify the ways in which need fulfillment might play out. Remember, appealing to core needs and applying DRM helps you cast the widest possible net to attract the largest potential audience.

The Seasons of Life from Wolfe's Ageless Marketing[49]

Spring: Initial Personal Development

The Spring of a person's life begins at birth and ends roughly around age 22. It revolves around a desire for play and includes a fantasy theme — a notion that generally, everything will work out "my way."

- *Developmental objectives* – Acquiring basic intellectual, emotional, and social skills needed to enter adulthood and navigate through it with reasonable success.

- *Developmental catalysts* – Persistent yearning for play through which learning takes place. The play imperative draws toddlers, older children, and adolescents into modeling life. Children and youth have the license to try roles, ideas, beliefs, and situations normally without fear of penalty for mistakes.

Summer: Social and Vocational Development

In the Summer of a person's life, between the approximate ages of 18 to 40, one is driven to become someone through work. In this season, people believe that the world is their oyster, swimming in the romantic theme that they can accomplish anything.

- *Developmental objectives* – Completing development of the social self, which includes integration into social networks (in the traditional sense, not necessarily in the online sense) and stepping into roles that serve one's vocational, social, and personal aspirations.

- *Developmental catalysts* – Yearning for work, the means by which a person satisfies a consuming focus on becoming someone socially and vocationally. Salaries support desires to make social statements that give material proof of a person's accomplishments; thus, Summer is the season of acquisitiveness.

Fall: Inner-Self and Spiritual Development

Around the age of 38, people transition into the Fall of their lives, where they begin to maintain a balance between their personal and professional lives. This period may include embarking on a search for meaning in life. Often, there is a sense of disappointment, brought on by the realization that life didn't work out exactly as expected.

- *Developmental objectives* – Advancing the inner self to a higher quality of self-expression, which involves its integration with the social self to yield a more resilient and balanced personality.

- *Developmental catalysts* – Yearning for life balance and meaning. The focus changes from becoming someone to being someone. The inner self, long submerged by an outer-world-directed agenda, aches for a simpler life. The quest for life satisfaction in Fall shifts progressively away from a focus on "things" to a focus on "experiences."

Winter: Becoming One with All

Reconciliation and acceptance are the primary motivators in the Winter of a person's life, which generally begins around age 58 and lasts through a person's death. There is an ironic overtone to this season because in making sense of one's life, people realize that there is some good in most bad situations and some bad in most good situations.

- *Developmental objectives* – Reaching a transcendent state that infuses one with a quiescence that both deepens life satisfaction and dampens the discomfiting impact of troublesome conditions the future may bring.

- *Developmental catalysts* – Yearning for reconciliation with the world, self, family, and friends. This is a time for squaring life's sweet moments with its bitter, for making peace with self and with all others.

Shifting from Spring/Summer to Fall/Winter

A significant event occurs as humans move from the Spring and Summer to the Fall and Winter of their lives. During this time, our biological makeup continues to change (remember that we are constantly growing) and we undergo a significant cognitive shift from predominantly absolute thinkers to more relative thinkers. People in the Spring and Summer of their lives generally see things in terms of black and white. They want facts and logic, and when asked to answer a question, their answers tend to be either yes, no, or one out of a list of options (think A, B, C, or D).

As adults move into the Fall and Winter of their lives, they begin to see the world in more relative terms. Their decisions are based on not only the facts, but also on the wealth of experiences they have accumulated up until that point, which forms a more holistic view of the situation. For more mature consumers, the answer is relative to the context and the situation, so the answer will "depend."

This shift toward more whole-brained thinking is one of the critical reasons for making an emotional connection with older consumers to survive information triage. Older adults will relate your message to a much wider variety of experiences and will draw their own conclusions based on those connections. (Leveraging this concept with conditional positioning is explained further in Chapter 6.) Keep in mind, however, that entering with an emotional approach needs that "follow-up punch" with the factual information. Because older consumers have shifted to become more relative thinkers, they still require the factual and logistical information to validate your product or service (in addition to the initial emotional connection).

The Necessary Shift in Marketing

Remember in Chapter 2 we said that one of the key ingredients missing in today's marketing campaigns was a deeper understanding of basic human behavior? Now, you can understand just what is necessary to gain that understanding and to better connect with boomer consumers:

- An understanding of both the biological and psychological factors that motivate consumer behavior.

- A holistic approach to marketing that shows consumers how you can help them fulfill their basic human needs.

- The recognition that, as we age, the manner in which we go about fulfilling those needs changes.

For example, let's take a look at Chico's, a store that has won the hearts of many boomer women.

Chico's Focus on Meeting Its Customers' Needs

Let's take a minute and first think about what needs Chico's is trying to fulfill for its customers. Clothing, fashion — it's all about how we look. In most cases, it is helping consumers fulfill their Esteem needs and meet their Identity values. Most women, regardless of their age, tend to be concerned with their appearance. How has Chico's made themselves so successful with boomers?

Many women, especially in mid-life and beyond, are self-conscious about their clothing size. Chico's has tailored its entire shopping experience around easing the often-painful chore of finding clothes that fit. It started by changing its sizing chart to a simple 0, 1, 2, and 3 (with half sizes in between). By employing an unconventional sizing system, it removes the stigma, and subsequent anxiety, from traditional sizes. (And frankly, even the largest size sounds small in comparison.) In Chico's, size is merely a number — it's all about how the clothes make a woman feel.

According to its website, "Focus on comfort is the reason for our unique sizing. There are many characteristics incorporated into each and every product we make, but top on our list is comfort. Chico's clothing is made to wear how you like it to fit. If you like a little room, go for a bigger size." Again, this simple statement takes the emphasis off of a woman's "size" and instead focuses on how the clothing, no matter the size, makes her *feel*.

Beyond its sizing chart, Chico's has implemented its philosophy into the retail experience. When you enter the store, you are greeted by sales associates who do not hesitate to share their own sizes and experiences with the clothing. There are no mirrors in the dressing rooms — further emphasis on comfort above all else. On its website, product descriptions from Chico's style expert, Sher, emphasize sexiness (without being overt), comfort, and practicality while simultaneously touting expressive color and style. And the website's "Pant Shop" wizard allows customers to find the pants that are the best for them in a friendly, unassuming manner, which is consistent with their emphasis on comfort. The message that greets consumers in this section says it all: "Finally…Pants that fit your body — not the other way around."

Chico's recognizes that Identity values and Esteem needs are more than skin deep. It transformed shopping into a peak experience focused on making a woman feel good about herself each time she shops at Chico's. If only all retailers viewed their consumers through this lens.

Applying the fundamentals of DRM to all of your sales, marketing, and customer service efforts will help you achieve a deeper, more meaningful connection between you and your consumers.

The Take-Away

The beauty of Developmental Relationship Marketing is that, unlike traditional marketing approaches, DRM is inclusionary instead of exclusionary. By appealing to the common needs of every individual, you invite the largest number of potential customers to engage with your brand on a deeper level.

- The key to connecting with consumers is not to try to identify their one, single need, but rather to determine what need(s) your product fulfills, and then make a connection with your brand's ability to fulfill the consumer's needs.

- Even though all of us share the same needs, the way we go about meeting those needs changes as we age.

- We can closely predict how someone might go about fulfilling their needs based on their season of life.

- As boomers move into the Fall and Winter of their lives, they transition from more absolute to more relative thinkers, making their view of the world much more holistic and experiential.

- By applying our understanding of human needs and how consumers, especially boomer consumers, go about fulfilling them, we can develop more cohesive and effective marketing campaigns.

Chapter 6:
Messaging and Imagery that Connects with Boomers

"We never knew what really to believe. Just word upon slogan with emotional connection."

— John Mellencamp, *"Country Gentleman"*

As you saw in Chapter 5, a significant cognitive shift occurs when people transition from the Spring and Summer of their lives into the Fall and Winter, broadly defined as a shift from more absolute to more relative and emotional thinking. This shift is not a linear progression, but instead results in a more holistic way of thinking, which allows older consumers to relate their wealth of past experience to what they currently experience day to day.

Remember in Chapter 2 when we explained that most boomers are dissatisfied with marketing? Much of this dissatisfaction might be rooted in marketing's lack of appropriate messaging and imagery. Messaging and imagery encompass the themes, words, sounds, and images you use to tell your story, integral elements in the unique approach to show boomer consumers how you can meet their needs. But before your products or services can fulfill their needs, boomers have to trust your company.

The Trust Factor

"Everything about your brand has to be trust-driven, familiar, and recognizable: your logo, your marketing, your language, your hiring policies, your management, your salespeople, your designers, your press releases, your advertising[50]," wrote Kim Brooks in 2001, for an article titled "Practicing Trust-Based Marketing." Becoming a trusted company means being trustworthy to the bone. However, you cannot make "trust" a marketing objective. Establishing and maintaining a consumer's trust is not as simple as sitting down for a brainstorming session focused on getting consumers to trust you. Rather, trust needs to be an outcome of genuine marketing that is backed by delivery on a promise.

Notice the critical word in the previous sentence: *genuine*. Don't underestimate the importance of transparent and authentic messaging when communicating with older consumers, and especially with the boomers. Since birth, baby boomers have been bombarded with marketing messages across a variety of ever-expanding channels — many of them feel like they have seen it all. And most boomers will tell you that they can spot insincere messages from miles away. Therefore, boomers will tune out and turn off insincere messaging much more quickly than other generations. And even if your message does ring true, you need to deliver on the promise to ensure that boomers continue to see your brand as trustworthy.

In recent years, social media has presented some of the most interesting challenges regarding building and maintaining consumer trust, especially for boomers. The following are some guidelines about boomer trust pertaining to social media that Jonathan has developed for us to share with our clients:

- *Make a commitment to be transparent* – Social media has taken the control of a company's message out of the hands of internal marketing departments and agencies and shifted into the hands of the consumer. (Breathe deep.) Many companies who have chosen to embrace social media avenues and who have committed to being transparent to their consumers have found that they've gained brand advocates from often-unexpected places. For example, consider Southwest Airlines' entry on their "Nuts" blog regarding the FAA's grounding of a significant portion of Southwest's fleet — and the resultant delays. While opening up this "can of worms" for discussion may send shivers up many corporate ladders, on this post, you will find not only harsh criticism of Southwest, but loyal customers, employees, and even vendors who steadfastly defend the brand. Southwest didn't take control. Rather, they chose to be a part of a conversation that was already happening.

- *Do not assume you control the information your audience can access* – Along the same lines as transparency, simply because your company does not supply certain information to the general public, does not mean that your consumers cannot access that information from other sources. In today's Internet environment, users are generating content about your brand and your audience will often access that information just as readily, if not quicker, than the official marketing materials you have so carefully released. Make sure you are delivering on the promise of your brand to ensure customers continue to have faith. And if you do have something to hide, consider how you'd handle that issue being brought to light. Or, could that be a proactive opportunity for you to be open and honest with your audience?

- *Recognize that social media users feel a sense of ownership –* This concept is one of the most important lessons we've learned when it comes to social media, especially with boomers. The type of interaction older consumers have through social media avenues can be more meaningful, introspective, and perhaps insightful to marketers than that of younger consumers. With age comes experience; boomers believe their opinions matter and are extremely vested in their online contributions. Not only do they have a sense of ownership of the content they produce through social media, they also are very loyal to the properties they regularly visit. Consider when Eons, one of the largest social networking sites for boomers, removed their age restriction of 50 or older and received some negative feedback from its members. In doing so, Eons had not changed their goal to build a boomer community. However, many users strongly felt that they, as creators of much of the sites' content, should have had some say in who had access to this site.

- *If you say you want feedback, mean it, and respond to it –* Again, this point reiterates boomers' sense of ownership and loyalty to the content they produce and properties they visit. Boomers' vested nature in favored social media avenues make them very likely to respond to solicitations for feedback. Does that mean you need to cater to their every thought? Definitely not. But if you are going to elicit feedback, do so with a genuine interest in what you may receive. And, if a major decision is an outcome (or not), it never hurts for you to be loyal to your users and explain the reasons for doing so. Regardless of a decision, at least it shows you're listening.

Another lesson to learn about boomer trust is their wariness of hype. As we have already mentioned, baby boomers have been exposed to more advertising than previous generations. They are not only very sensitive to broken promises, but also to advertising that tries to create a false sense of urgency or limit them in any way.

For example, flashing banner ads that offer "free" or extraordinary rewards rarely motivate boomers. In fact, most boomers will react negatively to a company that makes a claim with such a sense of immediacy. Likewise, boomers are skeptical of companies that make outlandish claims of being "the best" or "rated No. 1." Given their inclination to view things in relative terms, boomers will generally think that no one can claim to be the best because there are too many variables to be considered.

One of the quickest ways to lose consumer trust is by asking for too much personal information. Time and time again, Jonathan and I have seen seemingly genuine marketing efforts fall apart at the point of conversion or sale. This failure is often the result of a poorly executed attempt to gather the consumer's personal information.

While a company may have a vested interest in gathering a user's personal information, their users, especially mature users, may not place as much value on the product or information they are going to receive in return. For example, let's say you are offering a free guide on financial investments. So you ask a person to provide you with their name, phone number, address, email address, age, income, home ownership status, and marital status before you allow them access to the report.

From your perspective, this probably does not seem like an unreasonable request. All of this information will help you prequalify these leads. But look at the form fields from the consumer's point of view. They are likely early in the decision making process based on their request for preliminary information. They have not decided to invest and may not even want the information for themselves (maybe it's for their elder parent). For them, maintaining the privacy of their age, income, home ownership status, and marital status may simply be more valuable than your free guide, so they abandon the form and the opportunity for conversion is lost.

Be sure there is a balance between the value of your offering and what is being asked of a user to access it. Use tools like privacy policy links, security symbols, and affiliate organization logos, to help engender trust when you ask for personal information. There are also more subtle ways to show consumers why you are collecting certain data. Many website forms have a link titled "Why do we ask for this?" accompanying a certain field. Upon clicking on the link, users are provided with a genuine explanation as to why this information is needed.

Finally, don't forget, all of your online marketing touch points (including your website, micro sites, landing pages, ads, videos, etc.) must deliver on their promise and provide supporting information to back up any claims. Simply because older consumers are best engaged emotionally does not mean they will not require the factual information necessary to make an informed decision. It's imperative to remember the follow-up, left-brained punch once you get landing rights. As you read in Chapter 3, initially engaging older consumers through the right brain encourages them to eventually consume even more factual information than their younger counterparts.

The bottom line is that baby boomers are more likely to trust a company if they feel that the company understands them. In other words, they think the company knows what they need. Remember the primary need your brand fulfills? Showing a boomer that your brand can help them meet their needs shows them that you understand them.

Perhaps one of the best examples of connecting needs with a brand can be found in Match.com and its tag line "It's okay to look." Boomers are often at a disadvantage when it comes time to try to fulfill their Relationship needs. Because they are more inwardly focused, they may not participate in the same social scenes that help facilitate match making. Match.com is a Web property devoted to helping you find the perfect mate, but also addresses the insecurity that anyone, especially an older adult, might feel about online dating sites. "It's okay to look," it says. And it backs up this statement by providing helpful explanations of how online dating works and details on online dating safety. These tactics proved to be highly effective in connecting with mature consumers, especially when you consider that older daters drove Match.com's subscriptions to make it the largest dating site in the world[51].

Leveraging Word of Mouth

Word of mouth and peer recommendations are the most effective consumer motivator across all age groups, and especially for boomers. Boomers say that advice from family and friends is the most common way they research a new product and they believe that word-of-mouth recommendations from their friends, family, and peers is the most trustworthy source of information.

One simple way to leverage word of mouth is through the use of genuine, down-to-earth testimonials and user reviews on your website. In fact, during our usability testing at Immersion Active, we've found that such reviews and testimonials are highly valued by mature users. Our participants consistently cite that Amazon.com reviews are influential sources for product information. Enabling consumers to talk about your brand and allowing them to see what their peers have to say are powerful ways to promote your products. Likewise, boomers feel strongly that they must trust a company before they are willing to pass it on to their friends and families. And companies cannot ask for better-qualified leads than those coming from trusting advocates.

You can also increase the strength of your word-of-mouth recommendations by leveraging organizations that further validate the integrity of your company. Showing consumers that you are affiliated with trusted organizations such as the Better Business Bureau or a local Chamber of Commerce will boost the trustworthiness of your company in the mind of a boomer.

The one incongruence in word-of-mouth marketing with boomer consumers is the effectiveness of celebrity spokespeople. While older people tend to be more sensitive to accepting or rejecting famous personalities, our research has shown that boomers do value and trust endorsements from celebrities relevant to their own generation (i.e., celebrities who are boomers or seniors themselves). However, such endorsements must be presented in an authentic manner.

Consider Aleve's wonderful use of a famous personality:

A commercial for Aleve hurriedly opens with Leonard Nimoy, of *Star Trek* fame, walking through a backstage area talking on his phone: "Listen to me. You're my agent. You have to believe me. I can't do it. Why? Because it hurts!" Nimoy holds up his hand, fingers straight up with his palm facing the camera. Upon passing two younger fans who flash him the infamous *Star Trek* hand sign, he says, "I'm trying right now and it's not working. We'll have to cancel the date." He enters his dressing room, he sighs: "Aleve? Sure I'll try it."

Then, it fades to black. Nimoy walks onto a stage in front of an audience of anxious Trekkies. He holds his hand up, and with a triumphant burst of music, flashes the "live long and prosper" sign, fingers forming the "V" perfectly. As the audience goes wild, the narrator explains that, "Fortunately, just two Aleve have the strength to stop arthritis pain all day." The commercial simply ends with Nimoy reinforcing the tag line: "That's good news. That's Aleve."

 Read more online at
www.dotboombook.com/aleve

This commercial, whether you're a die hard Trekkie or not, is a quintessential use of a boomer icon endorsing a product. And while it features a celebrity, it also portrays a very realistic situation that boomers are facing: arthritis. But it does so with just enough humor to reassure viewers that Aleve is there to ease their pain.

The effectiveness of this technique may stem from the strong emotional connections boomers formed with these celebrities as they grew up watching television and going to the movies.

These emotions (remember, emotions elicit physical responses) make strong connections with boomers' right brains, leading to an increased likelihood of gaining landing rights and successfully surviving information triage.

The Cohort Effect

Before we move on, it is important to clarify a common term in boomer marketing — *the cohort effect*. From a marketing perspective, the cohort effect refers to the shared characteristics of a group of people. These characteristics result from common life events experienced during the time period in which the group has lived. For example, most boomers experienced the birth of television, the Vietnam War, the Kennedy assassinations, and more. Some marketing philosophies use these shared experiences as a basis to segment boomers. However, as we emphasized in Chapter 5, DRM is inclusionary, not exclusionary, yet obviously, generationally shared experiences impact people's lives. So how does the cohort effect work with DRM?

First, all humans share common core needs; however, how they go about meeting those needs varies by age and by cohort. So, not only will a 55-year-old go about meeting his or her Energy needs differently than a 25-year-old, but a modern-day 55-year-old goes about meeting her Energy needs differently than 55-year-old might have in the past. Even further, a 55-year-old will probably meet her needs differently in the future. While we will continue to biologically be more than 99 percent the same, it is our psychological differences that will continue to make us unique. In short, a person's life experiences play an important role in how he or she goes about meeting their needs.

For example, remember our 20- and 30-something employees who went running and played basketball to meet their Energy needs at our company retreat while our older employees read, played word games, and went for a walk? Well, today's boomer consumers might take that walk in their own backyard, but they are also very likely to take that walk while traveling to exotic destinations. Today's lifestyles are very different from those of 70 years ago; so how people go about meeting their needs varies greatly.

The Experience Economy

The "experience economy" has recently been the topic of many marketing discussions, blogs, and articles. Simply put, "today consumers increasingly desire neither goods nor services but sensation-filled experiences that engage them in a personal and memorable way. In the last two hundred years, society has shifted from an agrarian economy based on extracting commodities, to an industrial economy based on manufacturing goods, to a service economy based on delivering services, and now to an experience economy based on staging experiences[52]."

Today's consumers, and especially boomer consumers, are willing to pay for outstanding experiences. In fact, adults over the age of 50 account for 80 percent of all luxury travel spending[53]. And while economic influences may impact the affluence of these experiences, older adults are not simply kicking up their heels in retirement, relaxing once their children leave the nest, or sitting in the rocker on the front porch. Rather, they continue to seek peak experiences.

Second, and perhaps more important, a specific generation's life experiences often dictate what information gains landing rights in the conscious mind. Remember that one of the key factors in surviving information triage is the level of importance the unconscious mind places on a specific piece of information. The level of importance is often determined by how much other information the brain can relate to a new stimulus. So, if messaging and imagery are more contextual within a person's existing life experiences, the brain will perceive it as more important, thus improving the chances of gaining landing rights.

That's why, for example, songs invoke emotions. If you've been reading the introductory lyrics listed at the beginning of each chapter of *Dot Boom*, chances are you've already experienced this tactic firsthand. As humans, we cannot help relating songs with other previous experiences. As a result, our brains connect hearing that song with a previous feeling, which then evokes an emotional response. This automatic reaction is why so many marketers find nostalgic messaging and imagery to be effective with boomer consumers. (We'll talk more about the correct and incorrect ways to use nostalgia shortly.)

Evoking Emotions

As we established in Chapter 3, emotions are rooted in physical responses. So when marketing messages make an emotional connection, it can be extremely difficult for consumers to stop their brains from initially reacting. And because older consumers are generally more whole-brained thinkers who have a wealth of experience to relate to your messages, your chances of evoking an emotional response with them are significantly increased. Consider the following two landing pages that we developed for Home Instead Senior Care:

Landing pages from regional PPC campaign for Home Instead Senior Care.

The first version (A) of the landing page focuses on describing all of the features of Home Instead Senior Care's services. The text starts with a very left-brained approach to connecting with the audience:

> The Home Instead Senior Care® family of businesses helps older adults live comfortably and independently wherever they call home. Whether it's a few hours or 24 hours a day, we offer one-on-one, home care assistance with daily activities.

Compassionate, extensively trained CAREGivers™ provide help with:

Supporting older adults to live independently at home:	Benefits of our services:
Personal care	Allows aging in place at home
Meal preparation	Maintains independence
Medication reminders	Improves quality of life
Housework and laundry	Promotes a healthy lifestyle
Shopping and errands	Supports the family caregiving role
Appointments and outings	Provides peace of mind

To learn more or to schedule a free, no-obligation consultation, click on the map location nearest you or choose a location from the list on the right. Complete the Home Care Request form and a local Home Instead Senior Care representative will call you within 24 hours. You'll receive a free, no-obligation consultation to see if Home Instead Senior Care services are a good fit for your individual needs.

The second version (B) of the landing page takes a much more emotional approach to connecting with the audience:

Remembering Grandma's Sunday Dinners

Growing up, we had dinner at my grandma's house every Sunday. We'd walk three blocks down the street to her house, pausing to see what kind of new tree or shrub the neighbors had planted the week before. Mid-West style roast beef, fresh bread, coleslaw, green beans and gravy…every week. Somehow it never got old. You could smell the roast beef cooking from three houses away.

The minute I walked through the door I was hit with an explosion of familiar faces, the ever-present sound of the piano that never managed a perfect C, and warm, sweet smells of Grandma's kitchen. I'd always have to stop halfway through the kitchen for Uncle Chuck to tell the same joke with the same punch line — one that I'd heard a thousand times before.

I'd sneak a finger in the dark brown gravy and scoot out the backdoor before Grandma could swat me away. Out back, I was greeted by a motley group of uncles listening to Grandpa's stories, the clank-clank of horseshoes, and gray wisps of pipe smoke lazily drifting away.

Continuing My Tradition...

Sundays haven't changed after all these years. I'm doing most of the cooking now. My gravy still doesn't taste like Grandma's, but now I can taste test it any time I like. And somehow Uncle Chuck still manages to corner me with the joke I've never heard, or so he thinks.

Keeping Sundays the same isn't easy, but it's worth the effort, to continue our tradition. For you, maybe it's Sunday dinners. Maybe it's football games. It might be card night or Thursday evening television shows. It might be services on Sunday. Whatever they may be, everyone has traditions they'd like to continue, even if it takes the next generation twenty years to realize their appreciation for the green beans, Grandpa's stories, and even the jokes.

The version B continues with the story for another eight paragraphs before it gets to the call to action to inquire for service. Despite the fact that there is more content to consume before they get to the list of Home Instead services, a significant number of users completed the action from this version. We ran these landing pages as an A/B split and found that the emotional approach delivered a *52 percent conversion lift* over the standard, informational, left-brained approach.

 Read more online at www.dotboombook.com/home_instead

This finding is supported by the research I cited earlier from the Boomer Project, which found that when two advertisements were presented to study participants, the more emotional advertisement was preferred by an approximate three-to-one margin. Participants "said it did a better job of getting their attention and was more interesting and informative[54]." The emotional ad gained landing rights; people processed *more* of the information, even though each ad presented the *same* amount of factual information.

So what are the three strongest ways to make an emotional connection through marketing messaging and imagery? Storytelling, conditional positioning, and appealing to the senses.

Storytelling

If you stop to think about it, stories are one of the most effective ways to evoke human emotions. From childhood on, we love to hear stories. They make us happy, sad, excited, intrigued, scared, and content. Stories engage us.

But stories aren't simply told through text, especially online with its variety of interactive experiences — photos, video, games, calculators, and a vast number of other types of widgets can all be used to portray multiple facets of a story. And of course, in most marketing campaigns, you are not necessarily trying to tell a story in a "once upon a time" sense. Instead, you are conveying a message about a person, an event, and an outcome — in other words, an experience. By nature, humans relate to other human experiences.

Jonathan and I know that we are not the only ones hooked on storytelling. In a 2006 blog post, marketing guru Seth Godin wrote, "Great stories succeed because they are able to capture the imagination of large, important audiences. A great story is true. Not necessarily because it's factual, but because it's consistent and authentic[55]."

Consider the following description of the introductory animation on Harley-Davidson's website:

> A deep male voice begins with, "Over the last 105 years in the saddle, we've seen conflicts, recession, resistance, and revolutions. But every time, this country has come out stronger because chrome and asphalt put distance between you and whatever the world could throw at you." The sound of a signature Harley engine fades in while the narration continues. "And the rumble of an engine drowns out all the spin on the evening news. If 105 years have proved one thing, it's that fear sucks (and it doesn't last long)." Then, the sound of a motorcycle taking off blares while the voice proclaims, "So screw it. Let's ride."
>
> Text animates onto the screen during the narration, while strong words such as "conflict, recession, resistance, and revolution" pop out at the viewer, accompanied by

silhouettes of engines and muscles. The type is set on a gritty, yellowed piece of paper. In the background is an open desert road that leads to a mountain.

This animation presents a story, engulfing the viewer in a multisensory experience of riding a Harley-Davidson to escape from all the troubles in the world. It draws us in. We want to know what's going to happen, how the story will unfold and how it will end. It connects with our emotions of stress and fear. We can relate to the desire to simply get away from it all, in this case by hopping on a Harley. Most important, it positions Harley-Davidson as the solution to the problem — it empowers our escape.

Conditional Positioning

The key to successful storytelling in marketing, however, is to not tell the whole story in a literal fashion. Because everyone's experiences are different, if you tell a simple, straightforward story about a specific individual, a consumer may or may not relate to such experiences. However, if you include open ended elements, consumers can relate those to their own unique experiences, thus allowing them to insert themselves into the scenario. Consider our example above. In this case, virtually anyone can imagine themselves riding on the Harley, even Carol, Mary, or Robert. This technique of open-ended messaging is known as *conditional positioning*.

Cognitive research has shown that the human brain will finish incomplete pictures or fill in missing information based on personal experiences. Even more important, from a marketing perspective, consumers will fill in incomplete information in a way that benefits them. Try it.

Think about spending a night on the town with someone special. What happens during the evening? What do you do? Where do you go?

If you're like most adults, you probably finished the story with a pleasant dinner, meeting friends at a bar, or simply enjoying some entertainment. By nature, most people are unlikely to finish the story by thinking about a noisy restaurant with bad food or an unpleasant argument with your companion. Instead we'll "fill in the blanks" in a predisposed manner that is favorable to ourselves.

Borrowing again from Seth Godin's storytelling blog post: "Great stories are subtle. Surprisingly, the fewer details a marketer spells out, the more powerful the story becomes. Talented marketers understand that allowing people to draw their own conclusions is far more effective than announcing the punch line[56]."

In addition, when you force consumers to finish an incomplete story, they draw on their existing knowledge base, thus making more connections within their brain, which helps your messages not only survive information triage, but also become more memorable.

Finally, conditional positioning is the best way to allow consumers to insert themselves into a scenario because it presents your brand in a customer-centric manner, rather than with a product-centric focus. Through conditional positioning you make the messaging and imagery focused on the consumer and their needs, not on your brand and its features.

Imagery and photos can play a particularly important role in the conditional positioning of your brand because the photos need to invite consumers to insert themselves into the picture rather than showing someone else interacting with your brand. The photos and images need to be suggestive, rather than definitive.

Take a look at Corona Extra's website:

Can you picture yourself on a beach, ready to crack open a beer? I certainly can. This homepage is a great example of conditional positioning through imagery.

Not only can you insert yourself into this image, but if this beach isn't quite to your taste, Corona also offers a variety of others (see the thumbnail images and arrows below the main image) that you can choose to fit your personality and mood.

 Read more online at
www.dotboombook.com/corona

Appealing to the Senses

Using words and pictures that engage the five senses also elicits emotional responses our brains find hard to ignore. Think about the Corona homepage: the crack of a beer bottle opening (and the drinker's subsequent "aahhh"), the rush of the ocean breeze, the crash of the waves on the beach — all invite our senses to experience euphoric relaxation. For boomers, engaging their senses is especially important because, in their world, it is all about the sensations of the entire experience.

Homepage animation for Triple Creek Ranch

Immersion Active developed the website for Triple Creek Ranch, a lavish getaway in the Montana Rockies. After spending time at the ranch, we knew that its website needed to reflect the true feel of this luxury resort. The intro animation encompasses the serenity of nature, through the sounds of mountain winds and rushing streams, to the sumptuousness of the Triple Creek experience, by showing a crackling cabin fire and a mouth-watering gourmet dish. All of a user's five senses are engaged in this extravagant, dream-like display.

Read more online at
www.dotboombook.com/triple_creek_ranch

However, you do not have to simply rely on sight and sound. Words and images can suggest taste, touch, and smell that boomers will connect with their existing experiences. For example, consider the following text from a recent interactive campaign we developed for Del Webb, meant to appeal to boomers wanting to try new activities in retirement. "The soft sound of the brush running over the canvas. The feel of the paint tube between my fingers. I can finally connect with the artist within me." Through written words, we are engaging the senses and evoking an emotional response.

Even typography can convey the mood of a piece. In the case of a customer testimonial, for example, it not only provides a glimpse into that person's thoughts, but can also allude to their personality. For example:

We developed the following interactive journal for *AARP The Magazine's* website. It chronicles the adventures of a couple who, upon retirement, sold their permanent home to spend their retirement traveling the world. As part of this story, the couple sent a series of emails and letters back to the magazine editors. To help convey the sense of this story, we used a font with a typewritten look to convey the printed nature of this correspondence, which is combined with an email interface to underscore the electronic communication. The casual script font for the title of the piece, "At Home in the World," establishes a feel for the tone of the content and reflects the down-to-earth personalities of the couple.

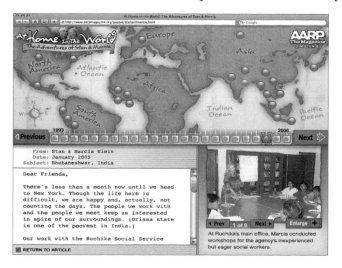

Read more online at
www.dotboombook.com/aarp

Animation and technology such as Flash features take static imagery to the next level as visual sources of engagement. The same applies for video. Our research has found that most boomers find online video highly engaging and very informative.

In fact, when we added video to selected pages on Home Instead Senior Care's website, we saw significant increases in the pages' effectiveness. Here is just one example: When we added video to the "Become a CAREGiver" page, the number of people who visited the "Apply Today" page (the page used to collect employee applications, one of the site's major goals) increased by 10.13 percent. The number of people who visited the "Find Home Care" page (the page used to start collecting service inquiries, the site's other major goal) increased by 15.36 percent. This jump was accomplished by simply embedding videos that Home Instead Senior Care had already posted to YouTube.

But It's Got to be Relevant

Storytelling, conditional positioning, and engaging the senses all enable messages to make an emotional connection. But none of that will matter if the consumer does not see your brand as relevant to them and their needs. Messaging and imagery need to be realistic, natural, and most important, genuine.

Too often marketers rely on stock photography or stilted messaging, neither of which represent the person whose needs marketers are trying to fulfill. And because older adults have had so many experiences, they quickly see through false, staged images of stock photography. Even worse, those campaigns are often viewed as ridiculous or inappropriate because they contain unrealistic portrayals of older adults. Boomers want to see and hear creative that reflects who they really are, and will react negatively to improbable scenarios.

Take a look at the following examples:

I hope it's obvious that the image on the right is most likely to appeal to a boomer woman interested in a golf outing.

If you want to connect with older consumers, simple tactics like using real images, not stock photography, or using photos where the subjects are not looking directly at the viewer, allow older adults to more readily insert themselves into a certain scenario. In addition, with regard to online images, the larger the image, the more likely the brain is to perceive them as real[57].

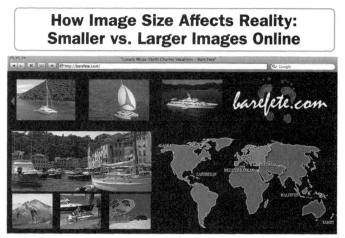

From Barefete.com: Smaller images don't connect in the same manner.

From BlackBook.travel: Larger images make the scene seem more "real."

At times, images that don't show full-body figures, particularly the face, may even be appropriate. Think about the Corona ads that only show the propped-up feet of two people lounging on the beach. The imagery in this advertisement is especially effective because those two people can be virtually anyone, as the images tell you nothing about the person's age, economic status, or even gender. At most, you might get a suggestion of ethnicity. Instead, these images focus on fulfilling a consumer's needs. In some cases, these needs may be Energy and Relationship. In others, it may be Esteem. Again, it's all relative because individual consumers see specific images fulfilling different needs.

Consider this example from a website we developed for Del Webb:

| Some users will focus on how the image meets Energy needs. | Other users will focus on how their Relationship needs are met. |

An individual looking to fulfill their Relationship needs might focus on the fun, social aspects of an artistic activity. But a person trying to fulfill Energy needs might focus on the rejuvenation they gain from artistic expression.

You can successfully connect with a wide variety of consumers through a single message or image because consumers will relate it to their own experiences. Ever heard that a picture speaks a thousand words?

Using Nostalgia Appropriately

So now let's return to nostalgic references, one of the most common ways to establish relevance with boomers. The key to using nostalgic references is making sure that they resonate with modern-day boomers. Too often, I encounter marketers who want to use images from the 1950s and '60s in their marketing messages, believing these images will automatically connect with a boomer's earlier experiences. It's true that these images may remind a boomer of their formative years, however most boomers will tell you that they want to see and hear about how they are living their lives today, not how they lived 30 years ago. Despite popular belief, most boomers don't long to be 20-something again.

I recently received an introductory video for the Touch of Gray website. Touch of Gray is a men's hair treatment that gradually dyes hair with each application, allowing men to preserve as much (or as little) of the salt-and-pepper looks as they'd like.

In the video, users are whisked into black-and-white, hippie flashback. The guitar riffs of the band Cream play in the background as the narrator opens with, "The generation that swore it would never get old...didn't." From there, viewers see older men surfing, partying on the beach, playing basketball, and performing in a band (and subsequently being kissed on the cheek by a young blonde with a tambourine).

Many companies fall into the trap of believing that all mature consumers reject their age and long for their 20-something lifestyles. But research has shown otherwise, even if Clapton is involved. In fact, most mature consumers rate their satisfaction with life much higher during midlife than any other time in their life.

Read more online at
www.dotboombook.com/touch_of_gray

Effective nostalgic references evoke positive emotions related to how boomers *felt* during an earlier period of their lives. They don't infer that the consumer would be better off if they were again living in that era or were that age. Simply playing music from the '60s and having actors rock out doesn't cut it. Boomers generally want to be portrayed as they are now — not as guitar heroes getting some love from a cute, young blonde.

But cultural icons that are relevant to boomer's lives today *do* work.

Roche Laboratories and GlaxoSmithKline use Sally Field as their spokesperson for BONIVA, a treatment for osteoporosis. Field serves as an authentic spokesperson because boomer women can relate to her as a cultural icon from their formative years, but also because she is speaking to them as a woman who is facing the same disease. Through the website (www.boniva.com), boomer women can sign up for MyBONIVA, a free program with reminders, a newsletter, and inspirational messages from

Sally Field. Using boomers within your campaign is effective, if you portray them as being relevant to the issues and concerns boomers face today.

 Read more online at
www.dotboombook.com/boniva

Other Effective Techniques

Some other techniques that work well for engaging boomers include the following:

Music – As I've already said, music can engage the senses and make an emotional connection with older consumers — it makes them listen. But, as exemplified by our Touch of Gray example above, simply playing classic rock in the background will do little more than make them tap their feet.

Positivity – Using positives over negatives is not just a matter of preferring optimism. "The brain processes negatives in two steps: first, thinking the positive and then applying the negative to it[58]." This even applies to the slightest use of negatives. For example, the call to action "do not hesitate to call" in a direct response piece would take twice the time to process when compared to the simpler and more positive "feel free to call." In fact, the older a person gets, the less likely they are to respond to negative messaging.

Demonstration – Generally, boomers would rather have you show and not tell. "You don't have to hit customers over the head with the point. You need to demonstrate things[59]." Less talk, more action, and remember to minimize the hype.

Intergenerational – It's impossible to ignore the cohort effect and the impact of life events. Mary, Robert, and Carol, along with their

78-plus million peers, are experiencing multiple life events at once, more than any previous generation. Many of these events revolve around family. Therefore, messaging that embraces multiple generations can appeal to these boomers who are becoming parents, grandparents, and empty nesters all within the same generation.

Leaving a legacy – Similar to the intergenerational appeal, boomers are reaching the season of their life in which they begin to think about the legacy they are going to leave to this world (fulfilling their Purpose or Identity needs). These desires are most immediately fulfilled through choices to shop green, invest in charitable ventures, or embark on a volunteer vacation. And messaging and imagery that fulfill a boomer's desire for altruism can be incredibly effective.

Gender clues – "Boomer women are getting more in touch with their masculine side and boomer men are getting more in touch with their feminine side. It's a biological fact. Traditional gender clues are less important to boomers at this stage[60]." We understand that most target consumer groups include both men and women, so reaching an androgynous middle point in the gender roles expressed in the creative usually works best for boomers.

The Take-Away

Now before you sprint to your creative department, designer, copywriter's office, or laptop, it's important that I reiterate a few key concepts in crafting boomer-appropriate messaging and imagery:

- A boomer consumer must trust your company before your marketing can truly influence them.

- Be genuine: If the messaging and imagery you create around your brand rings true and you do not deliver on your promise, you do more damage to your brand than if you did nothing at all.

- Make an emotional connection through conditional positioning, storytelling, and appealing to the senses.

- Be relevant to boomers as they are now. Use nostalgia thoughtfully — few boomers yearn to be 20 again.

Section 3:
Engaging Boomers Online

Now that we have a better understanding of what motivates boomer consumers, how do we leverage that knowledge to engage them with our brands? While many of today's seasoned academics, professionals, pundits, and gurus have made significant strides in developing and adapting marketing strategies to our ever-changing society, few, if any, offer actionable, implementable insight into how to create successful, replicable campaigns. When Jonathan and I decided to write *Dot Boom*, we knew we wanted our readers to be able close their eyes and envision how current marketing campaigns can change...for the better.

The beginning of this section marks the final part of the book. In Chapter 7, we'll explore a new, more boomer-friendly definition of engagement based on the important roles word-of-mouth and experiential thinking play in older adults' purchasing decisions. In Chapter 8, I'll share our Meaningful Online Engagement Model, a model we've developed at Immersion Active to create highly successful, integrated marketing strategies and campaigns that make an emotional connection with older audiences and have the inherent framework for replicable success across multiple channels. Finally, I'll close *Dot Boom* with Jonathan's and my personal thoughts on how you can inspire boomers to become influencers for your brand.

Chapter 7:
Online Engagement Redefined

"Long as I remember, the rain's been comin' down. Clouds of mystery pourin' confusion on the ground. Good men through the ages tryin' to find the sun."

— Creedence Clearwater Revival, *"Who'll Stop the Rain"*

Until we (at Immersion Active) developed a boomer-friendly definition of engagement – Meaningful Online Engagement – trying to measure how older adults were engaging with online media was like trying to follow a shadow in Times Square. We knew that boomers are active, engaged consumers online within specific media, such as video, email, search, and website browsing. On the other hand, when it comes to new media, such as Web 2.0, boomers are less likely to post comments, they're a minority among users of social networks such as MySpace and Facebook, and they represent only a small percentage of users who upload content on sites such as YouTube. But, we also know that boomers do still read blogs and view YouTube videos.

So how then can we quantify and describe the boomer's online level of involvement and interest, especially with regard to a specific brand or campaign? The problem has been the lack of a way to measure their level of *involvement* or type of *interest* cumulatively across the variety of online activities — hence, the need to re-evaluate advertising's effectiveness in relation to boomers.

Engagement – The New Marketing Metric

More and more, marketers are recognizing the need for a measurement of effectiveness that moves beyond the last action a consumer took. Instead, marketers are realizing that they need a measurement that provides a more comprehensive view of the variety of factors that influence consumer decisions. Recently, many experts have proposed that *engagement* is that new marketing metric.

Unlike page views, clicks, open rates, or transactions, engagement measures the interaction between the user and the site. It focuses on not only how often people visit a site and how much time they spend there, but also considers if they are leaving comments, writing reviews, blogging, and more. In other words, it places greater emphasis on how invested people are in the brand and their willingness to persuade others to support that brand as well. In turn, this knowledge allows marketers to try to influence that investment.

Measuring marketing effectiveness through engagement seems highly efficient. In fact, we wholeheartedly agree that you need to consider all of these factors when marketing to boomer consumers. But even this engagement metric fails to address some of today's most important marketing issues.

For example, this definition fails to consider *why* people are sharing and looking for information. What are the core human needs that are driving consumers' behavior? Today's definition also fails to adequately account for the exchange of information. It focuses primarily on whether a person generates sharable content — it doesn't adequately consider the movement of the information from author to recipient, the volume and velocity of that movement, or the credibility of the exchange.

In addition, this current definition of engagement does not consider where and how the information is exchanged. The places where content is being shared and the techniques used to share it play an equally important role in determining engagement. This definition falls short in recognizing that an individual's desire to influence others is only important in relation to the people, places, and things around them. One cannot simply analyze an *individual's* level of engagement but instead has to consider the cluster of people, places, and things that are either being influenced or trying to exert influence themselves.

The Evolving Conversation

Before the influx of user-generated content (one of the key components of "Web 2.0"), companies primarily generated the information consumers accessed online. A company had much more control over its online messages, which were delivered primarily through the brand's website, than it does now. In addition, online content was focused on information presentation (i.e., what you saw is what you got).

Today, however, the majority of online content is *not* being generated by corporate marketing teams. Rather, it's being created by the everyday consumer. People are posting pictures, writing reviews, rating products, joining blogs, and participating in online social networks like never before. Content has been freed from the confines of the page and from the control of individual companies. Subsequently, corporate content, displayed through technologies like video and widgets, now roams the Internet as tools for brand extension.

As a result, how we measure and connect with consumers online must adapt accordingly. We have to expand advertising opportunities to include an understanding of the multiple ways people are engaging in online conversations, instead of focusing on a single medium.

Consider this timeline and its three relevant perspectives:

Changing Perspectives from the Past 10 Years

PERSPECTIVE		10 years ago	3 to 5 years ago	Present
	Publisher	Should we be online? What should we include online?	How can I repurpose my content to be more interactive?	How can I leverage our content to extend brands (ours and our advertisers)?
	Advertiser	Where do I advertise?	What advertising formats should I use?	How should I advertise?
	Consumer	Where do I go?	How do I find it?	Who do I talk to? Who do I listen to?

Moving Toward a More Holistic Definition

It's important to note here that our definition of Meaningful Online Engagement goes far beyond the realm of simply analyzing user-generated content and Web 2.0 functionality. Rather, we are promoting a more holistic approach to online marketing that includes traditional online avenues, like websites, email and banner advertisements, as well as new media, like blogs, social networks, video, and widgets.

Moving beyond today's definition of engagement to a more holistic view is especially critical to effectively marketing to older adults. All consumers are trying to meet core needs, but older adults are more likely to tune out if your marketing campaign does not connect with those needs in an authentic manner.

I've already stressed that word of mouth is one of the most influential factors in older consumers' purchasing behavior. It's important to note that word of mouth is the *exchange* of information; it's not a one-way presentation of information, like a posting that someone may or may not read. In addition, if engagement requires exchanging information, then the places and technologies that enable that exchange play a critical role in successful engagement.

Finally, as we age and become more relevant, emotional thinkers, we evaluate marketing messages in relation to a lifetime's worth of experiences. We consider a wide variety of inputs and factors as we move toward a decision. Therefore, in order to connect with boomer consumers, we, as marketers, have to develop and optimize cohesive marketing campaigns that consider the holistic elements — people, places, and things — that make up our exposure to a brand.

A Better, Boomer-Friendly Definition of Engagement

What, then, is a better, more boomer-friendly definition of engagement? At Immersion Active, we define Meaningful Online Engagement as the exchange of information within a topic. A topic is a set of information focused on meeting one of our basic core needs. Meaningful Online Engagement is measured by monitoring things like relevance, intensity, attention, popularity, and authority — criteria we use to define influence. And you create Meaningful Online Engagement by developing marketing campaigns that integrate the creative messaging and imagery with the technology and media platforms used to deliver it (what we call the Campaign and Interaction Stories, which I'll cover in Chapter 8) to deliver a cohesive experience that inspires people to share the information with others.

Sounds like a mouthful doesn't it? Don't worry, I'll break it down and explain it in detail throughout the rest of this chapter. But before I do, I want to emphasize that this definition provides a way to measure the effectiveness and impact of marketing across multiple channels, platforms, and campaigns. It moves beyond simply asking if a consumer visited a website, posted a comment, or wrote a blog to also consider their investment in the information, their willingness to exchange the information, and their peers' responsiveness to the information that they shared.

By evaluating all of these areas, we can then determine how well our marketing efforts are influencing the information exchange. In the end, our goal is to become an influential force within any conversation (online or off). And by engaging with the various touch points that influence a consumer's actions, we can create a better campaign planning model that reflects the benefits of holistic marketing campaigns.

A Quick Summary of Meaningful Online Engagement

Meaningful Online Engagement is defined as the exchange of information within a specific topic, which is focused on a core need.

Meaningful Online Engagement is measured through:

- Relevance
- Intensity
- Attention
- Popularity
- Authority

Meaningful Online Engagement is created through integrated campaigns that inspire people to share information.

Exchanging Information

Meaningful Online Engagement is about exchanging information within a specific topic and aimed at meeting a specific core need or value. This distinction is critical to our definition of engagement.

In order for this type of engagement to occur, information has to flow. Like a river, it can surge, ripple, or simply meander along, but it requires movement. It is the passing of information between people, places (such as destination websites or social networks), and things (such as widgets and branded content) that creates engagement. More importantly, the exchange of information is focused within a specific topic and is driven by the desire for need fulfillment. Topics are exactly what you might expect; they are the subjects of the conversation. And the *need* is the motivation behind the information exchange — a reason to engage in the conversation.

Now you might think that the motivator for Meaningful Online Engagement is something as simple as the need to voice an opinion. However, we are actually referring to a deeper need, one of the basic human needs discussed in Section 2 of this book. If you take a moment to analyze any exchange of information, whether it occurs online or off, the exchange of information takes place to meet core needs. Let me share a real life example:

> Back in 2006, Jonathan and I were attending the AARP convention in California. At one of the displays was a restaurant-quality blender called a VitaMix, which lets you combine all types of ingredients to make a vast variety of foods, everything from soup to juice to ice cream. I spotted the VitaMix first and purchased one as soon as the salesman finished his demo presentation. (Confession: I can be a tad impulsive.) Immediately after, I raced across the convention floor, found Jonathan, and, after enduring some ridicule, dragged him back to watch the same demo. As you can guess, Jonathan, the less-impulsive one, also purchased one of the $400 beauties (much to the dismay of both of our wives).
>
> What makes this story interesting is the way in which the VitaMix meets different needs for each of us. For Jonathan, it's about meeting Energy needs because the VitaMix helps him eat healthier and prepare foods quicker. His Purpose needs are also fulfilled because, for the first time in his life, he can actually cook. (No more frozen pizzas for him.) For

me, it's about fulfilling my Relationship needs because it makes it easy to make ice cream for my wife and kids and soups for my friends during football season. This year, my brother, brother-in-law, and I are having a blend-off. I'm not kidding. (And I plan on winning.)

What's even more remarkable about this experience (and we're sure you've shared similar ones) is that we both continue to share our love of the VitaMix with our friends and family. If you ask Jonathan, he'll tell you that he shares his peak experiences about the VitaMix because he feels like it can help his friends and family eat healthier too. For him, it's about fulfilling his own Purpose needs by helping others. I, on the other hand, share my experiences with others so they can have similar peak experiences with their kids, which helps me strengthen my bond with friends and family, thus fulfilling my Relationship needs.

The same principle applies to online information exchanges. Someone posting a book review to Amazon may be primarily fulfilling an Identity need by positioning themselves as someone knowledgeable, while someone forwarding an email may be primarily fulfilling Relationship or Purpose needs.

In time, people will fulfill the need that drove their participation in a specific information exchange and they will move on to other exchanges focused on other needs. At the same time, new people, places, and things may move into the original information exchange. Over time, the nature of the information exchange will certainly change but because the core needs are universal and ever-present, focusing your marketing efforts on these needs keeps your brand relevant within the realm of online engagement opportunities.

So how do you position your brand within the information exchanges to show consumers how it can help to fulfill their core needs or values?

Defining Engagement Clusters

Exchanging information online is not that different from exchanging information offline. It's simply the platforms and channels used to exchange the information that differ. For example, an offline conversation might include being exposed to a television advertisement, talking to a neighbor over the fence (or multiple neighbors), talking to the salesperson in the store, and/or reading product packaging.

Online, this same conversation might play out through banner ads, peer reviews, white papers provided on a website, and product reviews on other websites. For tech-savvy boomers, these online exchanges can be as important to the conversation as a neighborly exchange over the fence. Each of these everyday activities has some effect (either consciously or subconsciously) upon our decision to act. Over time these multiple activities have a cumulative effect on the decision making process.

The Effectiveness of Cohesive, Multiplatform Campaigns

While it's widely agreed that multiplatform advertising is effective in increasing reach and brand recognition, it has also been proven that multiplatform advertising significantly increases conversion rates. Research conducted by Integrated Media Measurement Inc. (IMMI) in June 2008 compared the effectiveness of single-platform advertising to multiplatform for television and movie premieres. It found that even when conversion rates were controlled for frequency, the recency of exposure, and targeting, multiplatform advertising had a greater impact and led to higher conversion rates[61].

As you are beginning to envision the shape of your engagement opportunity, the key is to recognize and define the various touch points within the information exchange. Then, you can develop a strategy to use those touch points to influence the overall engagement level.

We call the sum of the various touch points and their information exchanges within an engagement opportunity a *cluster*. The various touch points within a cluster are called *nodes*, which are all the people, places, and things that enable the movement of information.

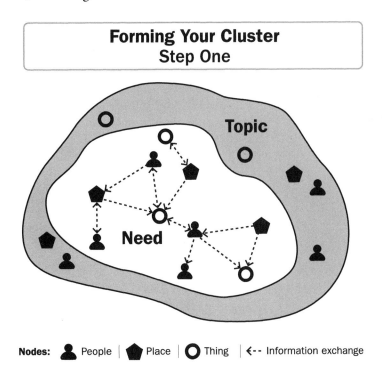

Forming Your Cluster
Step One

Topic

Need

Nodes: 👤 People | ⬠ Place | ⭕ Thing | ◀-- Information exchange

What distinguishes one cluster from another is the unique combination of topic, need, people, places, and things. Clusters are fluid and no two are exactly alike. They are not static entities that, once created, are rigidly defined and continuously exist. Instead, their participants move in and out as these needs are fulfilled or new needs become more pressing.

At the heart of it, clusters are simply loose networks for communicating word of mouth — making clusters especially effective for boomers. In boomer marketing in particular, receiving input from multiple sources, making connections to their existing knowledge and experiences, and passing that information on to others is paramount for success.

People, Places, and Things

For marketing purposes, *people* are the engine that drives the information exchange in a cluster. The places and things may be necessary to enable the flow of information, but people are needed to create and receive the information, and more importantly, to act upon it. After all, the end goal of the Meaningful Online Engagement opportunity (and marketing in general) is to get a boomer consumer to take a desired action.

Within the cluster, people include anyone who is participating in the information exchange. They are often boomers, but they may include people from any generation. These people may be creating a blog, posting videos on YouTube, writing a product review on a website, or sharing an email. At the same time, they also may be posting or reading comments on the blog, viewing or commenting on the video, reading a product review, clicking on an ad, or making a purchase. It is not only the content creators but also the content recipients who make up the cluster. As a marketer though, you want to identify the nodes whose audience seems most receptive to being influenced. That is a subtle distinction, as these are not influencers in the traditional sense (meaning they are not just a select few prognosticators or pundits). They can be sources you might not suspect. (More on influencers in a moment.)

But first, what about the places and things that make up the Meaningful Online Engagement cluster?

Places are locations where information is being exchanged. They can include websites, blogs, content-sharing sites like YouTube and Flickr, networking sites like LinkedIn, Eons, or Facebook, message boards, forums, and any other place where information can be exchanged online.

Things within the cluster include all the entities that help promote the flow of information. They could be an advertisement within a website, a calculator, or a widget. They might include technologies such as file uploaders, video viewers, or rating systems. And they certainly include techniques such as "forward to a friend" links, social bookmarking, and RSS. Things, in particular, are the enablers that help make the exchange of information possible. And most important, they make it easy. Like people, there are certain places and things that are more influential than others within your cluster.

Measuring the Intensity of the Information Exchange

Remember that our definition of engagement not only includes the exchange of information, but also gauges a consumer's investment in the information and the intensity of the exchange:

- Who are the people, including but not exclusive to boomers, who are passing along information?
- Who are the people, including but not exclusive to boomers, receiving the information?
- How receptive are they to the information?
- What is the perceived value of that information?
- Where is the information being passed?
- What kinds of things are being used to pass the information?

In order to accurately define, evaluate, and influence your cluster, you first need to be able to measure and monitor the information flow.

At the beginning of this book, we talked about the various ways marketers have traditionally measured the flow of information. Metrics, such as page views, unique visitors, time on site, and actions taken can all still help you measure the flow of information within your cluster, but in a very limited sense. Those metrics only measure the flow in a single direction and for a single point-to-point exchange. Likewise, even previous definitions of engagement (mentioned at the beginning of this chapter) focus only on measuring user-generated content — how many posts, reviews, or forwards an individual person contributes to the overall information exchange.

All of these other measurements fail to consider how information flows back and forth between nodes within a cluster (from point A to point B then back to A, or from point A to point B to point C). These measurements also fail to consider the role that the combination of specific people, places, and things plays in fostering the information movement. Measuring our more meaningful definition of engagement requires tracking more than standard analytics packages offer.

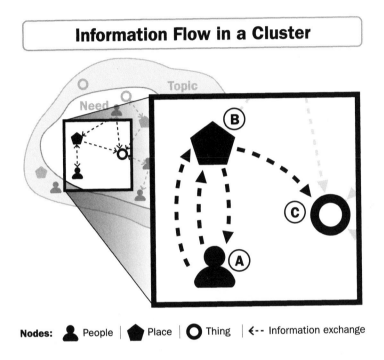

Information Flow in a Cluster

Nodes: 👤 People | ⬟ Place | ◯ Thing | ⬅-- Information exchange

Measurement Tools

So, how can you measure engagement? You are probably familiar with Web analytics tools that help you monitor the traditional, single-point metrics, but you may not be as familiar with other tools that help you monitor online conversations and the flow of information. Don't worry; you're not alone. Social media monitoring tools from companies like Collective Intellect, Techrigy, Visual Technologies, and BuzzMetrics continue to upgrade and expand their offerings for marketers who are concerned about monitoring their brand reputation online. Unfortunately, even combining these tools with your traditional Web analytics tools will not give you the complete picture you need to analyze your cluster.

Instead, to really measure the intensity of the information exchange, you have to use a combination of both quantitative and qualitative data. You need to know not only how many times a page is viewed, but, more importantly, if other people are forwarding that page to friends, social bookmarking it, or referring to it in a blog entry. You need to know what people are talking about on blogs and message boards in relation to your brand, and how passionately they are talking about it. You need to know not just who opened your email newsletter, but who thought it was so compelling that they forwarded it to five of their friends. In short, you need to know how many people took action based on someone else sharing information.

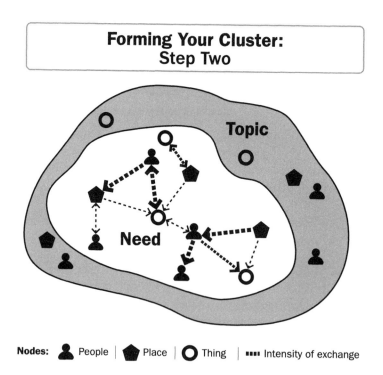

**Forming Your Cluster:
Step Two**

Nodes: 👤 People | ⬠ Place | ⭕ Thing | ▪▪▪ Intensity of exchange

To measure all of these factors, a combination of traditional analytics tools, newer social media monitoring tools, email distribution software tools, and some good old-fashioned research and evaluation is necessary. It isn't a purely scientific process, but it is a highly effective one. We'll provide you with more information and a framework for conducting this analysis and developing your strategy in Chapter 8.

In the end, what you'll arrive at is a more comprehensive view of the nodes that are affecting boomer consumer behavior. From there, you'll be able to identify the nodes that have the most influence — the ones that you, in turn, want to influence.

Defining Influencers

As we previously explained, within any cluster there are specific nodes that have a greater impact than others on the information exchange. These powerful nodes are what we refer to as *influencers*. They are the people, places, and things that help shape the conversation, leading it in different directions and motivating cluster participants to take action. The power of an influencer is generally measured in terms of its:

1. Relevance to the topic and need

2. Intensity of the information exchange in terms of both frequency and volume

3. Attention to the content from cluster participants

4. Popularity of the information they exchange about a topic, especially with regard to how often it is shared by others

5. Authority — the degree to which others refer to them as an influencer

The node's level of influence plays a significant role in helping you decide where and how you want to insert yourself into the cluster. Which nodes offer the best opportunities for you to inspire others to exchange information?

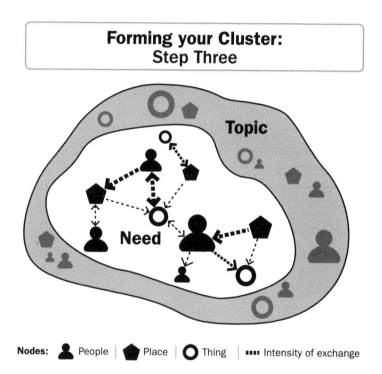

A common mistake is to believe that influencers are only the most vocal, active, or prominent people within a conversation. Recent research suggests that it is not necessarily just the most prominent spokespeople that can affect the conversation, but also the more numerous and active (but not necessarily leading) participants. This distinction is important. When evaluating your cluster, you don't necessarily have to, or even want to, try to influence only those few people, places, and things that are the most noted experts or the most prominent websites. Instead, you need to look at the cluster and identify the group of people, places, and things that together give you the greatest ability to influence the conversation.

For example, let's say your cluster focuses on healthcare reform (a specific topic focused on meeting Energy and Safety and Security needs). When you evaluate your cluster, you find it includes:

- A prominent doctor who has great visibility within the media and is a prominent spokesperson on health issues (a person);
- A monthly email newsletter focused on health and wellness issues with a subscription base of approximately 50,000 (a thing);
- A website totally dedicated to the topic (a place).

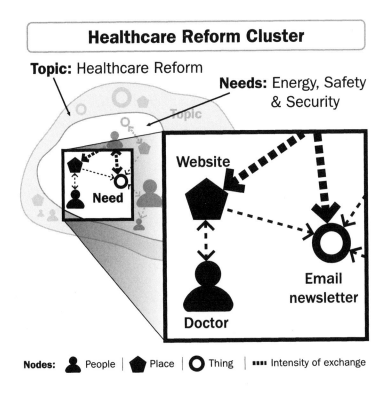

Healthcare Reform Cluster

Topic: Healthcare Reform

Needs: Energy, Safety & Security

Website

Need

Doctor

Email newsletter

Nodes: People | Place | Thing | Intensity of exchange

Let's first consider the website. Upon further investigation, you find that the content has not been updated in six months. It doesn't include any sharing tools, like a "Forward to a Friend" function or social bookmarking. Although it is very focused on your topic, it may not be the most influential node in your cluster. But what about the email newsletter or the doctor?

You might be inclined to try to target the doctor at first blush. He is well known and receives lots of media coverage. But is he really the most influential node? Recent research, and my own experience, suggests not. In 2007, CNET debunked the commonplace notion that a few, top-tier influencers reigned supreme over knowledge on a certain subject matter to inform the masses[62].

Middle-Tier Influences Are More Effective

Instead of trying to connect with the fewer, top-tier influencers, CNET's study concluded that influence is better modeled as a diamond, which places more emphasis on the middle-tiered influencers, rather than the top, elite few[63]. This diamond model of influence corresponds perfectly with our engagement cluster definition.

First, you have a larger number of nodes exchanging information. These nodes usually have more connections to other nodes, thus enabling even more information exchange. In the CNET study, they found a "high degree of correlation between self-reported influence activity and network size."

On average, the larger a person's social network, the more often they were asked for their advice, opinions, and so forth. In

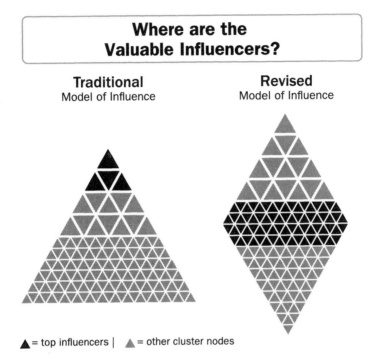

Where are the Valuable Influencers?

Traditional
Model of Influence

Revised
Model of Influence

▲ = top influencers | ▲ = other cluster nodes

other words, they pass along more information. (I should note that the CNET study only focused on social networks, which we consider only a part of an overall engagement cluster.)

At the same time, the CNET study found that technology (the "things" within the clusters) plays a greater role in connecting people with larger social networks. "Technology enables the maintenance and frequency of connections; obviously, it's easier to email 30 people about something than call them all individually. Thus, we see highly connected people making greater use of technology like email, instant messaging, and text messaging to stay in touch[64]."

The most poignant distinction CNET reported about these middle-tiered influencers is that influencers are motivated by a desire to help others. This notion goes against the commonly held belief that highly influential people are topical experts who impart their knowledge to demonstrate expertise. In fact, moderately connected influencers receive a sense of validation and self-worth (fulfilling Esteem and Identity needs) from advising others. They are taking time to impart their knowledge to those who need it, not simply sharing what they know with their entire network. And when their advice is well received, they become more motivated to expand their knowledge base. This motivation is especially relevant to boomers who seek and enjoy more peak experiences, and whose Relationship and Identity needs become more inwardly focused and altruistic in the second half of life.

So it is this more populated middle layer of influencers that may offer the best opportunities for inserting your message and impacting the conversation. These influencers are often viewed as more trustworthy and more reliable resources, especially for baby boomer consumers. To return to our example above, the health and wellness email newsletter targets the middle layer influencers with whom we would want to connect. Not only does it have a decent subscription base, but because it is an email, the information it can easily be shared and exchanged between many consumers, thus expanding its potential reach.

An Example of Meaningful Online Engagement

Before I wrap up this chapter on engagement, I thought it might be helpful to take a look at a highly successful engagement campaign — Dove's "Campaign for Real Beauty":

> When Dove began this campaign in 2005, most beauty product marketing relied on touting product features and

their effects on waifish, unrealistic models. To rejuvenate its marketing efforts, Dove went directly to its consumers and, by listening to their target consumers, discovered that women want reality — real women in real situations. More importantly, they want to be recognized as beautiful for who and what they are.

Dove launched its campaign with television advertisements that featured photos of women and asked viewers to go online and vote "Fit? or Fat?", "Wrinkled? or Wonderful?", "Grey? or Gorgeous?", and so on. The media was horrified, but everyday women loved it. In fact, Dove delivered more than 650 million media impressions in 2005 and more than 4.5 million unique visitors entered messages or blogged on Dove's website[65]. That's 4.5 million people who didn't just *visit* the website, but 4.5 million people who *engaged* in the conversation. And that doesn't count the millions of blog entries on other sites, millions of YouTube video views, or the numerous other social media sites developed around Dove's campaign (even including the spoof and critique videos developed and posted by consumers).

It's clear that consumers became engaged in this conversation, in this campaign, and with the Dove brand in a very intense way. And it worked. In a market space where growth was relatively flat, Dove was able to realize a 12.5 percent sales increase in 2005 and a 10 percent increase in 2006. "By consumer packaged goods standards, that is uncharted lift[66]."

Since 2006, the "Campaign for Real Beauty" has continued to expand. Today, if you visit Dove's website (www.CampaignforRealBeauty.com), you'll find tools for conducting workshops, a section for girls only, interactive experiences, blogs, tips, articles, expert advice, quizzes, and more. The company has even founded a Dove Self-Esteem Fund. (Oh, and one other thing you'll still find on its website: Dove product information.)

 Read more online at
www.dotboombook.com/campaign_for_real_beauty

Obviously, the "Campaign for Real Beauty" engaged consumers from a multitude of perspectives. They tapped into a cluster that revolved around Identity — a core need that was fertile for such interaction. If Dove had simply looked at the number of votes it had received for that first ad, it might have continued the campaign by simply creating more and more display ads along those lines. Instead, Dove realized that there was intensity within this topic that called for not only more ads, but also an exchange of information from the company and other participants. This exchange occurred on both its own website and others, using a variety of tactics and techniques. Measuring the effectiveness of this campaign goes far beyond simply looking at the votes received. Instead, it has to consider all of the ways consumers are exchanging information about "Real Beauty."

The Take-Away

Today many marketers have moved beyond simply rewarding well-performing ads to considering an individual's participation in social media and other brand interactions to arrive at a new definition of engagement. Their definition doesn't only count transactions but actually considers a person's willingness to create content about the brand. However, their definition still does not address many of today's marketing problems.

Instead, marketers need to employ a new, boomer-friendly, more holistic view of engagement, which is defined by the exchange of information within a specific topic that is focused on meeting a basic core need. This type of engagement can be measured by gauging the level of influence within the group of people, places, and things that make up the engagement cluster. By defining engagement clusters and identifying the influencers within those clusters, marketers have the opportunity to help shape the information exchange. When marketing starts to grasp those opportunities, brands are on their way to becoming influencers themselves.

Chapter 8:
A Model for Meaningful Online Engagement

"Tell me, what kind of man would I be? Living a life without any meaning."

— Chicago, *"What Kind of Man Would I Be?"*

In Chapter 7, I gave you a more boomer-friendly definition of engagement that allows you to build more holistic, more relevant, and more effective campaigns targeting boomer consumers. Now, I'll provide you with a way to consistently develop these engagement campaigns that are so critical to boomer marketing. The Meaningful Online Engagement Model (MOEM) was developed to provide marketers with a strategic planning framework that merges creative, media, and technical development into an integrated approach that will consistently result in more successful campaigns targeting boomers.

How many marketing campaigns have you seen that are terrific from a creative perspective but were lacking from an interactive standpoint? Or vice versa, have you come across an astoundingly useful interactive project, such as a financial services calculator, that lacked effective creative? The beauty of the MOEM is that it brings the interactive and the creative development together from the beginning to provide an integrated, cohesive process.

Let me say, however, that the MOEM is intended to provide you with a *framework* for developing your engagement strategy. It is not formulaic and there are no rigidly defined answers. It is simply a more systematic way to consider all of the components that make up successful engagement campaigns.

Using the Meaningful Online Engagement Model

As you employ the MOEM, you will develop three strategies that build on one another. Like a funnel, these steps should be performed in a progression in which the information determined in each step is refined in the next step. These strategies include:

- A *Brand Engagement strategy* – a sketch of the story you want to tell and the story in which you will be inserting your brand; and

- An *Audience Engagement strategy* – fleshing out the details of who you should tell your story to and how your story should unfold; and

- A *Content-Space Engagement strategy* – the finishing touches that result in an actionable, specific engagement plan for this campaign.

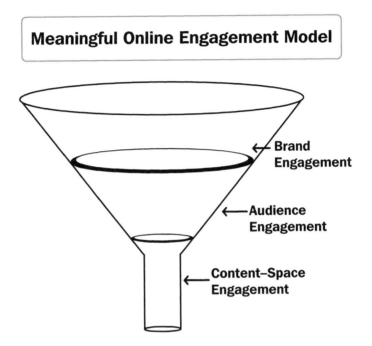

Meaningful Online Engagement Model

← Brand Engagement

← Audience Engagement

← Content–Space Engagement

As experienced marketers, you are probably already familiar with planning a brand and audience strategy. Chances are you have already been through the experience of determining the messaging and imagery you will use in your print, broadcast, radio, and perhaps even online advertising. You have probably already spent many hours working through the details of how your campaign will be delivered and to whom. If so, you may find many of these activities intuitive. But in order to truly engage boomer consumers, it's sometimes necessary to take a step back and consciously evaluate traditional strategies to ensure that campaigns are leveraging the effectiveness of needs-driven information exchanges, clusters and influencers, especially middle-tiered influencers.

Along the way, you'll go through a variety of planning exercises that will help you move toward a final, actionable campaign plan.

The outcome *may* include:

- A creative brief and a strategy brief from the Brand Engagement strategy

- Moodboard(s), creative concepts, interaction storyboard(s), and media concepts from the Audience Engagement strategy

- Creative content such as ads, articles, blog entries, etc. and a media plan from the Content-Space Engagement strategy

A key concept to note here is that, as you plan your engagement strategy, you will need to consider both your *Campaign Story* and your *Interaction Story*. Your Campaign Story is the story that you tell through your creative. It is the messaging and imagery and the forms those messages and images will take. The Interaction Story, on the other hand, is how your engagement plays out online through the users, Web properties, and tools used to exchange information. In order to create a holistic, thematic engagement experience, you need a strategy for *both* your Campaign and Interaction Stories.

In addition, we recommend that at least two people with complimentary skill sets work together to develop your engagement strategy: one who plays a creative role and the other who plays an interaction role. Note, however, that it is critical that both participants work together to develop all of the strategies, i.e., the creative person should not go off and create the Campaign Story while the other person develops the Interaction Story. Both roles need to actively participate in defining each element of all of the strategies in order to achieve the truly integrated campaigns vital to marketing to boomers.

Meaningful Online Engagement Model Scorecard

To help you as you build your engagement strategy, we have created a Meaningful Online Engagement Model scorecard that you can use as a tool to help gather thoughts, answer questions, and record data.

This scorecard can be found at our book website: www.dotboombook.com/scorecard

Brand Engagement Strategy Planning

 Your Brand Engagement strategy outlines how you want boomers to experience your brand online. I've stressed throughout this book that boomers are beginning to view the world more holistically; so integrated campaign experiences are most effective. But how will you unify the various, often disparate, campaign elements into a thematic whole — into a story?

In Chapter 5, we discussed that when presented with a partial story, the human mind will automatically fill in the blanks in a favorable manner. Think of each element of your campaign as a piece of that story, which becomes more complete as boomers are exposed to more and more pieces, in different formats. By planning a brand strategy, you can still allow for conditional positioning and consumer interpretation, but you are using your influence to shape that story to not only have a favorable outcome for the boomer, but also for your brand.

Because your Brand Engagement strategy is a story, it contains the same elements as any traditional story: conflict, setting, plot, characters, point of view, and theme. Granted, every aspect of your campaign does not play out like a literal "once upon a time" story;

however, planning each of these story elements is an important step in creating a more inclusive brand experience.

Brand Engagement within your Campaign Story

Many aspects of planning your Campaign Story are similar to activities you perform now, but with a slight twist. Let's take a look:

Conflict: The conflict within the story is the core need you are setting out to fulfill. Remember back in Chapter 5, I asked you to identify the basic need(s) you want to showcase your brand as fulfilling? That's the conflict you will resolve within your Campaign Story. (Note that it may touch on one or several core needs or values, depending on the campaign.)

Setting: The setting is the place and time you portray within your campaign. When marketing to boomers, setting can be especially important. Remember to use settings that are applicable to boomers' lives today, not necessarily a place or time from the 1960's or 1970's.

An equally important aspect of the setting is to consider the cultural zeitgeist: What are people talking about, especially in relation to the need you are going to fulfill and to the topic you are going to be discussing? Are there certain topics, images, or issues you need to avoid? More importantly, are there topics, images, and issues you cannot afford to ignore? These questions will play an important role in planning your Interaction Story, but they are also an important element of your Campaign Story. For example, if you are planning a Campaign Story for a new medical device, you cannot ignore the current political and societal issues surrounding the healthcare industry.

Zeit...what?

The term *zeitgeist* is a German expression that means "the spirit of the age." It is more literally defined as the intellectual and cultural feel of an era. The experiences of a dominant group of people within a culture define the zeitgeist, which in turn shapes a particular worldview of the entire culture.

August Everding, a German opera producer, once noted that the zeitgeist is an ever-evolving phenomenon that you must continually assess and adapt to. Everding emphasized his point by saying, "Whoever marries the zeitgeist will be a widower soon or in the near future," You can't assess the cultural zeitgeist and then assume it will never change. You have to go with the flow.

Interestingly, if you take a moment to consider it, you will see that the baby boomers have managed to define our culture's zeitgeist at practically every stage of their lives. When they were in the Spring of their lives, we experienced a revolution in child-rearing approaches and educational approaches (think of Dr. Benjamin Spock and open classrooms). As boomers entered the Summer of their lives, American culture became youth-centric. Remember the motto "Trust no one over 30"? Now as boomers are moving into the Fall of their lives, we are again seeing a shift in the zeitgeist toward more socially conscious, greener, legacy oriented endeavors and activities.

Plot: The plot is the sequence of events that allows you to determine your basic theme — a theme that needs to be connected with your boomer audience's core needs. As you plan your Campaign Story, remember that you are planning a series of information exchanges, not a single, one-time advertisement. This sequential nature of information exposure allows you to initially make an emotional connection. Then you can follow-up with more logical information, thus securing landing rights in the conscious mind of an older consumer.

When developing your plot, consider the following elements:

- Introduction – What messages introduce your brand to your target consumers? How do you make it relevant? How do you get landing rights?

- Rising action – What resources can be made available to make the information in the story most relevant to your target boomers? More importantly, what can you provide that will build suspense and desire?

- Climax – You've built the suspense, the tension, and the desire, so what is that penultimate moment where a consumer balances on the precipices of action or inaction? What messages and images do you need to push them up and over this precipice?

- Falling action – What action do you want boomers to take and how will you encourage that action? What messages, calls-to-action, and other techniques will you use in your creative to encourage action?

   Remember, the action does not have to be immediately purchasing your product. Purchasing decisions are a progressive process, so the next action you want someone to take might be passing the information to a friend, going to another location to find out more information, or calling to set up an offline sales appointment.

- Resolution – Were the consumer's needs satisfied? More importantly, have you given them a peak experience that makes them want to return to your company again and again, share their experience with others, and become an advocate for your brand? Boomers aren't necessarily the brand loyal boomers we once thought they were, but they are very *experience-loyal*, returning or staying with brands that continue to meet their needs and provide them with peak experiences.

Characters: When planning the characters within your Campaign Story, remember to use conditionally positioned, relevant characters. Boomers need to be able to relate to the people within your campaign and, unless you want to create an unlimited number of campaign variations for all types of people, the best way to encourage this relationship is by using conditional positioning (see Chapter 6 for more on that messaging and imagery concept). And if you use real characters, they have to be relevant to boomers as they are today, not as they were 30 years ago. Finally, as your plot progresses, your characters should also progress. If you want consumers to move toward a goal throughout your campaign, your characters need to continue to grow as well.

Point of view: The point of view for your Campaign Story is relatively simple; it is the perspective from which the story is told. But again, this perspective is very important with regard to how it allows your consumers to relate to your brand. If you simply present information in absolutes or "black and white" terms, chances are that boomers are going to say "not necessarily" or "it depends." Boomers' referential and experientially-based thinking requires that you tell your story from a conditional point of view.

Theme: The theme for your campaign is the culmination of all of the story elements. In determining your theme, ask yourself: "What do I want someone to walk away with after experiencing my brand?" Your theme needs to be tied to the primary need your product fulfills and focused on culminating in a peak experience. It is crucial to evaluate if boomers felt like your brand delivered on its promise and were motivated to exchange information about your brand with one another.

This approach to developing your Campaign Story allows you to transition from a fragmented to thematic approach for developing your Brand Engagement strategy. By encompassing each element of the story, your campaign elements will be unified into a holistic online brand experience.

Brand Engagement within your Interaction Story

Similar to the Campaign Story, your Interaction Story needs to consider each of the traditional story elements, but through a different lens:

Conflict: Within the Interaction Story, the conflict is the same need you are fulfilling within your Campaign Story, but specific to how it plays out online. What need does your product fulfill that boomers are exchanging information about online? In addition, when planning your Interaction Story, you need to consider the emotions that are tied to this need and how are they being exhibited online. Are people really excited about a new innovation that helps them meet their need? Are people angry about a political movement or lack of resources to meet that need? Are people sad, confused, curious, or anxious? Considering the emotions that are tied to these needs will help you shape both your Campaign and Interaction Stories.

Setting: Again, setting is a place and time, but instead of being the place and time you portray within your Campaign Story, it is the place and time where you insert yourself into the online conversation. Where, when, and how is information being exchanged? Or more accurately, because you are in the beginning stages of planning your engagement strategy, what kinds of places and things will you want to influence within your cluster? You do not need to identify specific properties and techniques at this point in the plan, but you do need to consider what nodes of a potential cluster would most likely be influential and how you would influence them.

And, as with the conflict, do not forget to consider the emotional aspects of place and time. Where are people displaying or sharing their emotions? When and how?

Plot: As with the Campaign Story, remember that you are planning a series of information exchanges, not a single, one-time event. So, how will you encourage information exchange through your cluster from point A to point B to point C, or back and forth between two points?

Again, consider the following elements:

- Introduction – Where might you first introduce yourself into the cluster? How will you do that in an authentic, trustworthy, non-threatening manner?

- Rising action – What actions or information exchanges will you encourage or participate in to move a consumer along? Where do they need to take place? What things can you contribute to the cluster that will keep the information flowing?

- Climax – What can you do to push a consumer to that precipice? What information or things can you provide, in the places you identified in your setting, that will motivate someone to action?

- Falling action – How will you enable a consumer to take the next step? Where and how will you facilitate that fulfillment of their need? Just as in your Campaign Story, within your Interaction Story, what does that action really need to be? (Note: It does not necessarily have to be an immediate purchase.)

- Resolution – What "things" can you do to continue their peak experiences, enable boomers to share their experiences, and encourage them to become a brand advocate?

Authenticity

Before we move on, it's vital to point out the importance of authenticity and trustworthiness in your information exchanges, especially as your plot unfolds. Just as the phrase "as the plot thickens" conveys, the methods you use to move your story forward can easily be misconstrued as self-serving hype. Consumers, and especially boomers, are extremely sensitive to corporate information that seems focused solely on making the sale. And they are even more sensitive to information that appears to be disguised as genuine but turns out to be a marketing ploy. For example:

In September 2006, Walmart shoppers and RV-enthusiasts were introduced to Jim and Laura through a blog titled "Walmarting Across America." It began innocently enough — upon purchasing an RV, an older couple decided to travel around the country visiting their three adult children. In passing a Walmart parking lot one night, they discovered that the chain allows RVs to park in their lots for free.

And so their journey and blog began. But less than a month later, Jim and Laura's love for Walmart became a bit suspicious. A subsequent investigation by Business Week Magazine found that although Jim and Laura were real people on a trip, the blog was actually a promotional tactic from Working Families for Walmart, an organization that was launched by Walmart's public relations firm. What's worse is that the organization paid for the RV and all travel expenses. Jim and Laura were mere pawns in one big online publicity stunt — a stunt that tarnished Walmart's online image.

So, as you insert yourself and your story into the clusters, make sure that you are authentic and transparent. First and foremost, you must truly provide value and help a boomer move toward the fulfillment of their need. If your brand is not going to help them achieve their goal of meeting their need, don't say it will. Boomers will find out in the end and the negative stigma that results will do much more damage to your brand than any initial uptake in sales can counter.

And even if you truly can help them fulfill their need, make sure they know who you are and what your goals are. We've all heard about marketers who have posted comments to blogs under false names or paid people to post positive reviews (a minor offense compared to Walmart's aforementioned misstep). These tactics simply do not work. Participating in the conversation as yourself shows boomers that you truly do want to help them and that, as a company, you are not afraid to let them see the real you. Authenticity and transparency are critical to successfully marketing to boomer consumers, especially online.

Characters: The characters within your Interaction Story are the people within your cluster. Again, you are still in the first of three stages of your engagement strategy; so don't worry about analyzing all the possible demographics, metrics, and social media conversations at this point. Instead, you want to focus on the *types* of people you want to leverage within your cluster (think of them as personas). Who might make up that middle influencer layer? How and why are they exchanging information? What can you do to engage them and encourage them to pass along your information?

Point of view: The point of view for the Interaction Story is the reference from which the information is presented. It could be omniscient (a leading, authoritative source), third party opinion (a blog), omniscient objective (Wikipedia), first person (your company itself), or stream of consciousness (open forum postings). Which point of view will work best within the different settings and with the different characters within your cluster? Which point of view do you need to use as your plot unfolds?

Theme: Finally, like the Campaign Story, the theme for your campaign is the culmination of all of the Interaction Story elements. How does your brand story play out consistently across the multiple channels and platforms? What is the overall brand experience that results from the various touch points and interactions within your cluster? Does your brand story provide for a cohesive, holistic encounter?

Now that you've planned your Brand Engagement strategy, you have a whole list of thoughts and ideas about how your brand story will play out online. Allow me to stress that the development of both Campaign and Interaction Stories within this strategy should not happen within a vacuum; they benefit most from back and forth between the different skill sets within your team. The end result of the Brand Engagement strategy may include creative and strategy briefs that include thoughts on messaging and imagery, interactive elements, potential cluster participants and how the campaign will play out online, i.e., interaction opportunities.

Now it's time to hone and narrow that strategy into something actionable. The next step in the MOEM, the Audience Engagement strategy, helps you start to refine these ideas into a more coherent plan.

Audience Engagement Strategy Planning

Your Audience Engagement strategy is what you will use to identify the more specific nodes of the cluster you want to influence and where, when, and how you insert your message into the conversation. It's at this stage that you will start to employ the variety of tools to measure the intensity and participant investment in the information exchange.

Unlike the Brand Engagement strategy, which started with the Campaign Story, we'll start with the Interaction Story because what is determined about the target audience in the Interaction Story affects the Campaign Story.

Audience Engagement within Your Interaction Story

In your Brand Engagement strategy you identified the need your product fulfills (conflict), the types of people who are exchanging information (characters), the places and things they are using to exchange information (setting), how and when you will insert yourself into the information exchange (plot), and the overall impression you want people to walk away with (theme).

Based on this information, you need to investigate the more specific information exchanges that are occurring and build off of the characters you defined in the Interaction Story within your Brand Engagement strategy. Using traditional metrics tools, social media monitoring, email tracking tools, and research, you need to answer these types of questions:

- What conversations are happening online around this need? What is the topic of these conversations?

- How much information is being exchanged about these topics?

- When is it being exchanged? And more importantly, how long has the exchange been going on and how long might it continue? In other words, how quickly do you need to enter into the information exchange and how agile does your engagement strategy need to be?

- Who is exchanging the information?

- Where are they exchanging it?

- How are they exchanging it?

- How is the plot currently unfolding during the information exchanges?

- What are the most up-to-date societal norms and influences that you need to be aware of as you insert yourself into the information exchange?

Remember that answering these questions is not just about monitoring social media. It's also about looking at the websites people are using as resources, the tools they are using to access the information, and the techniques they are using to exchange the information. Most important, it's looking at how the information is moving between the different nodes in the cluster and which pathways have the most intensity. In the Audience Engagement strategy, we are *not* testing for click-thru rates; we're aiming for pass-thru rates — essentially trying to determine where the highest Audience Engagement is in relation to your brand. Once you've answered these questions, you can move on to analyzing your Campaign Audience Engagement Story.

Audience Engagement within Your Campaign Story

Once you know where, when, how, and at what level of intensity information is being exchanged, you then overlay that strategy with your Campaign Story to refine the types of creative messaging and imagery you need to develop and the forms that it will take. Ask yourself questions such as:

- Given the places where conversations are happening, what types of creative might you need? Will you need to create blog entries, post comments, add factual information to your website, generate articles to post on other websites, create a widget to be included in multiple locations, produce a video, or create a banner ad?

- Which of these types of creative are the best "things" to encourage information exchange? Are there other tactics and techniques, such as forward to a friend or social bookmarking, that you should include in your creative to help foster sharing?

- Will you need different types of creative as your plot unfolds?

- Which types of creative will work best for the people in your cluster?

- What specific messages will work best and what point-of-view do you need to use to convey those messages?

- What images and graphical elements are best for this cluster?

- How will the messages and images change as your plot unfolds? Will they change across the different types of creative? If so, how?

- Are all the elements cohesive and representative of your theme?

Answering these questions, and others like them, allows you to end your Audience Engagement strategy phase with a set of planning tools such as: moodboard(s), creative concepts, interaction storyboard(s), and media concepts (a high-level outline of the types of places you will be targeting). You'll also see that at this point, the funnel is getting narrower, and the Campaign and Interactive Stories are merging.

One additional item to consider during your Audience Engagement strategy is testing and optimization. It is during this phase of the MOEM that you can start to actually test your thoughts and ideas in the real world. Develop sample creative and place it in sample locations. See what happens. No matter how many metrics you evaluate, how many experts you consult, or how much research you do, I can guarantee that you will learn something new by actually putting your ideas into action through limited testing and seeing how your cluster reacts.

Content-Space Engagement Strategy

Your Brand Engagement strategy helped you develop the story you want to tell. The Audience Engagement strategy determined whom you should tell your story to. Now, the Content-Space Engagement strategy will help you implement a specific approach for each type of influencer in order to most effectively motivate them. It is where the Campaign Story and the Interaction Story merge to become one cohesive engagement story.

As you plan your Content-Space Engagement strategy, answer these questions:

- Who are the most influential people and what are the influential places and things in your cluster?

- What specific messages and images work best with these influencers?

- How can those messages and images be displayed in a way that captures the campaign essence and evokes emotions in the boomer (while staying true to the brand)?

- How can you best insert your messages and imagery into the cluster to most effectively connect with these influencers?

- What combination of influential people, places, and things will allow you to have the greatest impact on the exchange of information?

- What do you need to do to specifically get these influencers to exchange your information?

- What do you need to do to specifically get people in your cluster to take action?

- What frequency will engage but not overwhelm your influencers?

- To what level should you actively participate in the conversation or let others move the conversation forward with only your guidance?

The answers to these questions will allow you to create a specific implementation plan that includes a media plan and all of the creative materials necessary to execute that plan. This implementation plan details the people you want to connect with; the places you want to participate in the conversations; the tactics and techniques you want to use to participate; the messages and imagery you want to use; and the formats they need to be in. In other words, you will have a marriage of your creative, interactive, and technology that results in a thematic brand experience. You will also have planned your engagement strategy.

Do I Have To Do This Every Time?

Having read through this explanation of the MOEM you may ask yourself, "Do I have to go through all of these steps all of the time?" Well, just as most older consumers would say — it depends.

When considering which of the above activities to perform, you need to consider the risk and the reward. How large is your campaign budget? How new is your brand? When was the last time you completed all of the steps? What can you afford to skip and what can't you? Only you can truly make these decisions, as each engagement opportunity is going to be unique.

I suggest that you at least briefly review your Brand Engagement and Audience Engagement strategy each and every time. What does "review" mean? Ask yourself if there have been shifts in the conversation or in societal norms that need to be considered. The depth of your review is dependent on the risk and reward of investment. And I recommend you always re-establish your Content-Space Engagement strategy. The fluidity of the Internet demands that you always analyze the best influential opportunities for each new campaign.

The Take-Away

Online influence must be exerted through a cohesive set of Brand Engagement, Audience Engagement, and Content-Space Engagement strategies. Together these three strategies present the thematic, holistic brand experiences that are most effective with boomer consumers. As you build your three engagement strategies and unify them into an online marketing presence, you may achieve another laudable goal: becoming an online influencer yourself.

Becoming an influencer allows you to become one of the thought leaders whose ideas are organized, integrated, and supported by third-party references to an extremely influential degree. What's more — you can inspire influence in your target consumers.

Chapter 9:
Inspiring Influence

"Come on baby light my fire. Try to set the night on fire."

— The Doors, *"Light My Fire"*

In the first chapter of this book, I suggested that marketing (in a sense) is broken. Its youthful, product-centric, metrics-centric focus has caused subsequent efforts to become ineffective. As a result, it has overlooked the most powerful group of consumers in the U.S. — the baby boomers. And many of the marketers who now recognize the potential of this consumer group are at a loss when it comes to effectively motivating their buying behavior. However, the harmonious combination of DRM and Meaningful Online Engagement strategies will result not only in more successful campaigns, but also in transformative and profitable relationships with your target consumers.

By combining DRM with a strong engagement strategy, you can create holistic, meaningful online marketing campaigns that do more than just connect with older consumers. By actively engaging them, you help them to fulfill their biologically- and psychologically-driven, basic human needs. This fulfillment can then lead to the ultimate satisfaction — peak experiences.

Delivering on this promise of fulfillment requires a high-tech, human-touch approach. It is high-tech in the sense that the Internet offers a plethora of opportunities to deliver your message and allows you to monitor and measure your engagement campaigns like never before. At the same time, it requires a humanistic approach to that delivery, which is needs based, relevant, and contextual, and makes emotional connections necessary to gain landing rights.

This process requires employing these high-tech and human-touch approaches in the appropriate places, at the appropriate time, with the appropriate people. Borrowing an analogy from Duncan J. Watts, professor of sociology at Columbia University: "You don't necessarily devote your energy to sparking a particular tree as much as identifying the places that have the right conditions for a blaze." You need to focus on finding the right combination of conditions that will invoke a flurry of information exchange and participation in that exchange, rather than devoting all of your energy to developing that one sparkling advertisement, in order to truly start a fire.

Gathering the Kindling

Finding the ideal conditions to start a fire means identifying where you can insert your brand into the conversation in the most potent manner. How can you determine what touch points and conversations have the most potential for your brand? The answer is often to find those conversations that have the most emotional connections revolving around them. These areas may be the ones where people perceive a threat to their ability to fulfill their needs or where there are conflicting needs among multiple groups. Being able to elicit powerful, positive emotional responses with your brand is the pinnacle of not only marketing effectiveness, but also influence.

Not only do you need to evaluate where the most potential is for a fire, but also where your brand is going to be most relevant in starting and building that fire. It may sound obvious, but relevance is especially critical with boomer consumers. Remember, they are more whole-brained, experiential thinkers who are going to determine whether to accept or reject your information based on its relevance to their own life experiences and values.

A key factor in that evaluation is their perception of the authenticity and trustworthiness of your information and your brand. The more a boomer trusts a company, the more likely they are to not only buy, but also to pass information on to others and promote the flow of information. Word of mouth is the most important boomer marketing tool, but you will not generate word of mouth about your brand unless the boomer consumer sees you as relevant, genuine, and trustworthy.

And finally, look for that middle layer of influencers where there are more people, places, and things being used to exchange more information. Targeting a few high-profile influencers, like a bright flame from a single burning tree, may be seen from miles around, but unless the conditions exist for the flame to spread, it will soon burn out.

Being the Spark

So now that you've found where the people, places, and things are that you need to start the fire, what truly enables you to become the spark that sets it off and the arid wind that keeps it moving?

In an insightful post[67] on his blog Micro Persuasion, Steve Rubel delves into the book *Tiger Traits* (written by Dr. Nate Booth), which identifies Tiger Wood's key traits to success. Within his blog Rubel viewed these traits "through a Web 2.0 lens." We'd like to take his thoughts one step further and look at them through our DRM and Meaningful Online Engagement lens:

Identify and develop natural talents: To become an online influencer, identify the touch points most pertinent to your specific campaign over which you can have the most influence. As Rubel advises, "pick your spots and play to your strengths."

Create a clear and compelling dream: Remember, boomers are turning to your brand to help them fulfill a need. Make it clear and compelling how your brand will do so, and make sure it is honest and true.

Select teachers, heroes, and teammates who guide, inspire, and support: In this case, the point is simple — select the influencers who will not only influence, but who will also guide, inspire, and support you and your brand.

Be confident: "Most people who are opinion leaders online are extremely confident." The campaigns you are producing through DRM are helping boomers process their lives, no matter what brand, product, or service you are promoting. Believe it. If your marketing efforts are authentic and genuine, then project confidence in the voice of your messaging.

Manufacture a magnificent mental model: The many conversations happening through ever-evolving media can be overwhelming. But "if you figure out what to tune in and what to tune out, you will succeed. Skip the gossip. Unsubscribe from the blogs that do nothing but spew smoke. Frown on distractions." Your goal is to inspire the influencers; do not allow yourself to get distracted.

Let actions do the talking: As new media is being developed, so are new metrics to measure and monitor every aspect of it. While the Web offers campaign monitoring like never before, do not let yourself get too hung up on sheer numbers. If you consistently create solid, authentic campaigns for which you have matched the needs of your consumer with the needs your product fulfills, you will rise to the top. Then, you can allow the numbers to speak for themselves.

Consistently improve in good time: Crafting developmentally-based, engaging campaigns will provide stronger, more effective results. But remember, your engagement clusters are in a constant state of flux. People move in and out, places are built and taken down, and newer things replace older ones. Just because your initial engagement strategy was successful does not mean it will continue to be. You need to consistently re-evaluate your engagement strategies and application of DRM to continue to provide peak experiences.

Igniting Your Own Spirit

As two marketing professionals in the late summer of our lives, Jonathan and I caught a bit of flack from our (sometimes ageist) industry peers when we established our niche of solely focusing on the 50-plus markets online. To those unaware of the power of mature consumers, it seemed almost contradictory that we could leverage ever-evolving, high-tech interactive media to engage older adults online. However, we know that the Internet offers revolutionary avenues for marketing to further the conversation between brands and their consumers. And it only made sense to focus our efforts on the most underserved consumer group. (Madison Avenue had the rest covered.)

But if you're like us, to truly fulfill your own needs, you'll have to accomplish more than successful marketing campaigns. Just like boomer consumers (and anyone else we've mentioned in this book), *you* have Identity, Purpose, Relationship, Energy, and Adaptation needs to fulfill.

Let me share with you what has transformed the way I view my profession:

Purpose: Helping your brand succeed and seeing it help mature consumers meet their core needs will provide a greater sense of purpose and meaning. For me, it has made my role as a marketer less of a job and more of a calling.

Identity: Obviously, being successful and making money helps, but beyond that, DRM and engagement-based marketing can help you meet your self-awareness, self-preservation, and self-image needs, as well as gain the respect of others.

Relationship: For me, the harmonious combination of DRM and Meaningful Online Engagement strategies has resulted not only in more successful campaigns, but also in transformative relationships with Immersion Active's target consumers and our clients. Emotional connections and shared goals can help you build connections you've never before been able to realize.

Energy: While there's no denying that implementing any advertising campaign can be exhausting, I have found that the deep, meaningful connections I make with Immersion Active's clients, co-workers, or consumers, revitalize and energize me in a profession where many marketers feel beaten down and frustrated.

Adaptation: Because the DRM-Meaningful Online Engagement approach includes an iterative, repeatable, and systemic process for producing successful boomer marketing campaigns, it provides me with the skills I need to continually adapt to the changing Internet, marketplace, and audience.

Of course, neither Jonathan nor I would ever go so far as to suggest that marketing can end war, solve hunger, or possibly fulfill all of your basic human needs. But if marketing to older adults is truly broken, Developmental Relationship Marketing and Meaningful Online Engagement offer you the opportunity to be both an important and inspiring part of the solution.

Appendix:

Appendix A:
Where Are They Online?

In evaluating where boomers are going online, it is best to first look at it from a site category standpoint. It is important to understand that there is no one standard pertaining to types or categories of Web properties. There are quite a few lists out there, but they are varied. For the purpose of this book, I decided to categorize websites by their related industry, since Immersion Active focuses primarily on business-to-consumer websites.

Site Categories

A list of the top website categories (ranked by advertising dollar amount)[68] is as follows:

1. Multi-service portals/search engines/IP
2. Business/finance/investing
3. News/current events
4. Sports
5. Local news/guides
6. General interest/entertainment
7. Computing/technology
8. Movies/video/TV/cable
9. TV stations

10. Search engines
11. Games
12. Health/fitness
13. Travel
14. Internet service provider
15. Automotive
16. Cards and screen savers
17. Common cultures/communities
18. Music/broadcast/radio
19. Real estate
20. Shopping
21. Special interest/hobbies
22. Food
23. Meeting places
24. Hispanic
25. Education/reference

Hitwise data from July 2006 showed five categories strongly represented by Internet users over the age of 55: Pharmacies, eGreetings, Cruises, Gambling/Games, and Entertainment Competitions[69]. While the first three categories may not surprise you, the last two might.

Many boomers are experiencing increasing health concerns as they age. In fact, 82 percent of adults who use the Internet research health and wellness information online[70]. An important aspect to consider is that while boomers may be researching on behalf of themselves, they may also be looking into the health concerns of an aging loved one. In recent years, baby boomers have been coined as the sandwich generation, because many are stuck in between caring for their children and caring for their aging parents.

Previously, we mentioned that email remains the most popular online activity for boomers; so sending eGreetings is a natural extension of their growing desires to keep in touch with friends and family. In regard to travel, 42 percent of all luxury travel purchases happen online, with adults over the age of 50 accounting for 80 percent of all luxury travel spending[71].

However, what often surprises marketers is that online gaming and entertainment websites have become quite a phenomenon among older users. Casual gaming sites (like Pogo.com), which are usually one-player and easy-to-learn, are most popular with boomers. These can include activities like board games, puzzles, and simulated casino games. Older users spend a significant time on gaming sites, with an average of 10 to 20 minutes[72]. In fact Hitwise found that in June 2006, visits to gaming sites made up 2.6 percent of all Internet visits — a significant percentage in relation to the total number of websites that exist.

Likewise, boomers are drawn to gaming sites that may help improve their cognitive fitness. According to a recent report from marketing research firm SharpBrains, the brain fitness software market reached $225 million in revenues in 2007. For many boomers, this is not solely an entertainment-driven activity. Many have watched their parents struggle with Alzheimer's disease and are now seeing themselves as vulnerable to degenerative neurological diseases. Rather than sitting by the wayside, they are taking action for prevention.

In addition to the five types of websites outlined above, baby boomers also spend a significant time online looking for love. Dating websites, such as Match.com and eHarmony.com, have seen a surge in older users in recent years. Another popular dating site, LavaLife.com, recently launched LavaLife Prime, an online dating service exclusively focused on people age 45 and older. Many boomers unabashedly tout that their increasing age does not hold them back sexually. The New England Journal of Medicine found that while the prevalence of sexual activity decreases with age, men and women still have sex well into their 80s and 90s. In fact, sex after 50 remains one of the most popular community discussion topics on both Eons.com (one group is subtly named "Hot Tub") and ThirdAge.com, social networks geared toward 50-plus users.

I've covered the kinds of sites that are most popular among baby boomers, but I know you want specifics. So what are the specific Web properties that are most popular among baby boomers?

Top 50 websites among users of all ages (ranked by reach) and ages 50 to 64 specifically (ranked by reach and by composition index)

All ages	Ages 50 to 64	Ages 50 to 64
By reach*	By reach*	By composition index**
Google.com	Google.com	AARP.org
Yahoo.com	Yahoo.com	PCH.com***
Live.com	Live.com	RealAge.com
MSN.com	MSN.com	SocialSecurity.gov
Wikipedia.org	Wikipedia.org	QVC.com
AOL.com	AOL.com	Accuweather.com
YouTube.com	YouTube.com	Wunderground.com
MySpace.com	MySpace.com	Breitbart.tv
Microsoft.com	Microsoft.com	Legacy.com
eBay.com	eBay.com	NOAAwatch.gov
WordPress.com***	WordPress.com***	NewsMax.com
Mapquest.com	Mapquest.com	HSN.com

All ages	Ages 50 to 64	Ages 50 to 64
About.com	About.com	VA.gov
Blogspot.com	Blogspot.com	iWon.com
Facebook.com	Facebook.com	ADN.com
Craigslist.org	Craigslist.org	SSA.gov
Time Inc. sites***	Time Inc. sites***	Breitbart.com
Ask.com	Ask.com	HGTV.com
Typepad.com***	Typepad.com***	DrudgeReport.com
Go.com	Go.com	BlueMountain.com
Answers.com***	Answers.com***	EverydayHealth.com
PhotoBucket.com	PhotoBucket.com	FamilyLink.com***
Adobe.com	Adobe.com	Fidelity.com
Imeem.com***	Imeem.com***	Scottrade.com
Information.com	Information.com	WCBSTV.com
CNN.com	CNN.com	Townhall.com
WordPress.com	WordPress.com	TXLottery.com
Windows.com	Windows.com	Vanguard.com
CBS.com***	CBS Network	SurveyRouter.com
PayPal.com	PayPal.com	Topix.net
Blogger.com	Blogger.com	Fool.com
FederatedMedia.com	FederatedMedia.com	CBSNews.com
Walmart.com	Walmart.com	CNBC.com
Widgetbox.com***	Widgetbox.com	KHOU.com
Comcast.net	Comcast.net	Bloomberg.com
ATT.com	ATT.com	NorthernTool.com
Flickr.com	Flickr.com	GreenfieldOnline.com
Lotame.com	Target.com	Vendio.com
Target.com	Weather.com	AP.org
Weather.com	Geocities.com	ZDNet.com
Geocities.com	RockYou.com	Mercola.com
RockYou.com	IMDB.com	DoNotCall.gov
IMDB.com	Bizrate.com	Grisoft.com
Bizrate.com	ReverbNation.com***	JoshHosler.biz

All ages	Ages 50 to 64	Ages 50 to 64
ReverbNation.com***	Nabbr.com***	WorldNetDaily.com
Hulu.com	BankOfAmerica.com	Intermarkets.com
Nabbr.com***	YellowPages.com	BookingBuddy.com
BankOfAmerica.com	WhitePages.com	AmericanGreetings.com

This data, from Quantcast Media Planner, is ranked by users of all ages and users age 50 to 64. What's interesting is that when ranked by reach, the top 50 sites for users of all ages are not that different from the top 50 sites for users age 50 to 64. What is different is the concentration of older users in specific places, indicated by the composition index, often on smaller sites.

This trend poses some unique questions for media planners. Should you target smaller sites with higher concentrations of boomers or should you target sites focused solely on boomers? The answer to how to effectively craft your media campaign is dependent on building an overall campaign strategy that focuses not only on where boomers are online, but also on what they are doing, why they are doing it, and how to influence their actions. In other words, it depends on your engagement strategy.

 For more updated data, visit
www.dotboombook.com/top_50_sites

* Data representative of a 12-month period ending November 14, 2008. Reach is defined as a measure of the number of people visiting a site over a set period of time. Quantcast's reach figures are in relation to a calendar month.

** Data representative of a one-month period ending November 14, 2008. Composition index is defined a measure of how a certain figure compares to an average. The higher the index, the better the site is at attracting the type of audience specified by the figure[73]."

*** A hosted network is defined as multiple websites that are hosted under one domain. For example, Wordpress is a hosted network because its domain includes all of the blogs people have created on the site.

Appendix B:
Developmental Relationship Marketing Model

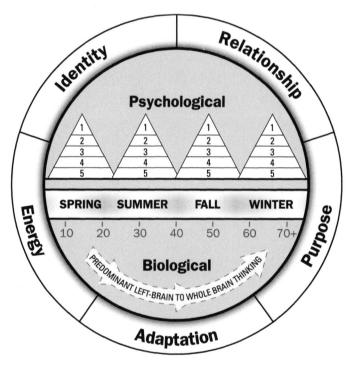

1=Physiological | 2=Safety & security | 3=Love & belonging
4=Esteem | 5=Self actualization

This illustration shows the holistic nature of Developmental Relationship Marketing by encompassing all of the theories discussed in Section 2 of this book. Together, both the biological and psychological realms of our thought patterns motivate consumer behavior. As all humans age, we progress through the seasons of life: Spring, Summer, Fall, and Winter. A significant shift in thinking occurs between the Spring/Summer and Fall/Winter transitions — a shift toward more whole-brained thinking, which encompasses both the left (logical and rational) and right (impulsive and emotional) sides of the brain. Throughout our lives, we are motivated to fulfill each of the needs in Maslow's Hierarchy of Needs in a linear fashion. Thus, we are constantly striving to move up the pyramid once lower level needs are basically fulfilled. However, we experience all of Wolfe's core values throughout our lives, regardless of age, season of life, or level of Maslow's hierarchy.

Appendix C:
Web Resources

Throughout this book, I have referenced numerous campaigns, case studies, and resources that exemplify the theories and strategies of *Dot Boom*. Visit the book's website, www.dotboombook.com, for a more in-depth look at the referenced materials. Here's a glimpse into what you will find:

1. Man-on-the-street interviews with boomers in my hometown of Frederick, Maryland

2. Kleenex's "Let It Out" campaign

3. Landing pages developed for Home Instead Senior Care by Immersion Active

4. Kashi Foods website

5. Flash intro animation developed for Triple Creek Ranch's website by Immersion Active

6. "At Home in the World: The Adventures of Stan and Marcia" interactive piece developed for AARP by Immersion Active

7. Corona website

8. Aleve commercial featuring Leonard Nimoy

9. Intro animation for Harley-Davidson's website

10. "Touch of Gray" video on the Just for Men website

11. Boniva campaign featuring Sally Field

12. Elements of Dove's "Campaign for Real Beauty"

13. Immersion Active's proprietary Meaningful Online Engagement scorecard

Glossary

Branded content – A form of advertising that blurs conventional distinctions between advertising and entertainment or education; the most notable form is product placement, but common online components are helpful articles or widgets that are subtly branded by the advertiser *(initial reference on page 111)*

Campaign Story – The story told through marketing or advertising creative *(initial reference on page 134)*

Cluster – The sum of the various touch points and the information they exchange on a certain topic, which is focused on a specific core need or value *(initial reference on page 114)*

Cohort effect – The common characteristics a group of people because of to shared life experiences *(initial reference on page 80)*

Conditional positioning – Open-ended form of storytelling that allows and invites consumers to insert themselves into a scenario presented in advertising messaging *(initial reference on page 69)*

Hosted network – Multiple websites that are hosted under one domain name; example is the blogging network WordPress because numerous blogs are hosted under the WordPress domain *(initial reference on page 168)*

Interaction storyboard – A map of the various technologies used for the Interaction Story of a marketing or advertising campaign *(initial reference on page 134)*

Interactive Story – How the campaign story plays out online; the technologies that enable the creative *(initial reference on page 174)*

Moodboard – A visual tool for representing the creative direction of a Campaign Story; may include images, text, and sample objects *(initial reference on page 134)*

Nodes – The various online touch points (of people, places, and things) in a cluster *(initial reference on page 115)*

Reach – A measure of the number of people visiting an online destination over a set period of time *(initial reference on page 114)*

Rich media content – Online content that incorporates audio, animation, or video; synonymous with interactive media *(initial reference on page 14)*

RSS – Acronym for Really Simple Syndication; enables publishers to distribute content quickly or automatically through a standardized format that reproduces frequently published works, such as blog entries, news headlines, audio, and video *(initial reference on page 16)*

Sandwich generation – A term coined for the baby boomer generation, as many are "sandwiched" between caring for their children and elderly parents *(initial reference on page 164)*

Social media – Any online content based on user participation or user-generated content; examples are social networks, blogs, and forums *(initial reference on page 14)*

Social media monitoring tools – Online programs that measure and monitor user participation and user-generated content online *(initial reference on page 119)*

Web analytics – Process of collection, measurement, and analysis of user activity to understand their behavior online and better achieve marketing objectives *(initial reference on page 119)*

Web 2.0 – Trend that aims to facilitate collaboration and information sharing among online users; lead to the development of social networking websites, blogs, wikis, etc. *(initial reference on page 105)*

Widgets – Portable pieces of code that can add dynamic content to any HTML page; generally used for advertising or branded content purposes, e.g., a retirement calculator sponsored by a financial services company *(initial reference on page 26)*

Zeitgeist – The intellectual and cultural feel of an era *(initial reference on page 137)*

Endnotes

Preface

1   Hertzberg, Robert, Angela Pugh, and Claudine Singer. "The Graying of the Net: Broadcasters and Publishers Should Exploit Their Built-In Advantage." Jupiter Research, 2000.

2   Musico, Christopher, "The Boomer Boom." DestinationCRM, November 1, 2008. www.destinationcrm.com/Articles/Editorial/Magazine-Features/The-Boomer-Boom-51407.aspx

3   "The State of Retailing Online 2008." Shop.org and Forrester Research, September 2007.

Chapter 1

4   U.S. Census data

5   Dictionary.com, www.dictionary.reference.com/browse/baby (accessed August 19, 2008).

6   Dictionary.com, www.dictionary.reference.com/browse/boom (accessed August 19, 2008).

7   Dictionary.com, www.dictionary.reference.com/browse/baby%20boom (accessed August 19, 2008).

8   "Boomers: The Next 20 Years." Institute for the Future study, 2006. www.iftf.org/node2056.

9   "Current Population Survey." Annual Social and Economic
     Supplement, U.S. Census Bureau, 2005.

10   "Current Population Survey." Annual Social and Economic
     Supplement, U.S. Census Bureau, 2005.

11   Vann, Korky. "More Seniors, Boomers Going Green."
     The Cincinnati Post, July 5, 2007.

12   K. Davis. "Oldies but Goodies." U.S. News and World Report,
     March 6, 2005.

13   "Survey of Consumer Expenditures." U.S. Bureau of Labor
     Statistics, 2006.

14   "Survey of Consumer Expenditures." U.S. Bureau of Labor
     Statistics, 2006.

15   "The Employment Situation: September 2008." U.S. Bureau of
     Labor Statistics, 2008.

16   "The Employment Situation: September 2008." U.S. Bureau of
     Labor Statistics, 2008.

17   "Survey of Consumer Expenditures." U.S. Bureau of Labor
     Statistics, 2006.

18   "When are the peak earning years?" The Financial Engineer Blog,
     February, 23, 2008. (Accessed November 7, 2008:
     http://thefinancialengineer.blogspot.com/2008/02/
     when-are-peak-earning-years.html)

19   Hertzberg, Robert, Angela Pugh, and Claudine Singer.
     "The Graying of the Net: Broadcasters and Publishers Should
     Exploit Their Built-In Advantage." Jupiter Research, 2000.
     www.jupiterresearch.com/bin/item.pl/research:concept/63/id+84643.

20   "ISPs Need to Satisfy Older Market Segment." InternetNews.com,
     April 4, 2000. www.internetnews.com/stats/big_picture/
     demographics/article.php/5901_334031.

21   Verna, Paul. "Baby boomers and silver surfers: Two generations online." eMarketer, December 2007.

22   "SIMM media consumption study." BIGresearch, 2007.

23   Finch, Kerry. "Online Habits of Baby Boomers." EzineArticles.com, March 25, 2008. www.ezinearticles.com/?Online-Habits-of-Baby-Boomers&id+1066178.

24   Verna, Paul. "Baby boomers and silver surfers: Two generations online," eMarketer, December 2007.

25   "North American Technographics Retail Online Survey." Forrester Research, 2007.

26   "North American Technographics Retail Online Survey." Forrester Research, 2007.

27   "North American Technographics Retail Online Survey." Forrester Research, 2007.

28   Verna, Paul. "Baby boomers and silver surfers: Two generations online," eMarketer, December 2007.

29   Finch, Kerry. "Online Habits of Baby Boomers." EzineArticles.com, March 25, 2008. www.ezinearticles.com/?Online-Habits-of-Baby-Boomers&id=1066178.

30   Kim, Gary. "Boomer Broadband: Boom!" IPBusiness.com, July 1, 2007. www.ipbusinessmag.com/departments. php?department_id=3&article_id=52.

31   "Boomers Big on Word-of-Mouth." eMarketer, March 21, 2007. www.emarketer.com/Article.aspx?id-1004709.

32   "Boomers Big on Word-of-Mouth." eMarketer, March 21, 2007. www.emarketer.com/Article.aspx?id-1004709.

33   Verna, Paul. "Baby boomers and silver surfers: Two generations online," eMarketer, December 2007.

34 Verna, Paul. "Baby boomers and silver surfers: Two generations online," eMarketer, December 2007.

35 "The promise of social network advertising." eMarketer, December 2007. www.emarketer.com/Article.aspx?id=1005688.

36 "Does Ur Granny Text?" InsightExpress, September 18, 2007. www.insightexpress.com/release.asp?aid=371.

37 "So How Big is RSS Usage Online?" The Mobispine Blog, October 29, 2007. blog.mobispine.com/2007/10/so-how-big-is-rss-usage-online.html.

38 Rainie, Lee and Jeremy Shermak. "Search Engine Use Shoots Up in the Past Year and Edges Toward Email as the Primary Internet Application." Pew Internet and American Life Project and comScore Media Metrix, November 2005.

Chapter 2

39 "Baby Boomers Upset TV Isn't All About Them." MSNBC.com, November 28, 2006. www.msnbc.msn.com/id/15806591.

40 "Baby Boomers Uniquely Positioned to Embrace Emerging Entertainment New Media, TV Land's Joy of Tech Study Finds." PRNewsWire, January 2, 2008. www.sev.prnewswire.com/entertainment/20070102/NYTU10602012007-1.html.

41 As according to the theories of David Wolfe and Abraham Maslow.

Chapter 3

42 Zaltman, Gerald. How Customers Think: Essential Insights into the Mind of the Market. Boston: Harvard Business School Press, 2003.

43 Wolfe, David and Robert Snyder. Ageless Marketing. Chicago: Dearborn Trade Publishing, 2003.

44   Wolfe, David and Robert Snyder. Ageless Marketing. Chicago: Dearborn Trade Publishing, 2003.

Chapter 4

45   Wolfe, David and Robert Snyder. Ageless Marketing. Chicago: Dearborn Trade Publishing, 2003.

46   Wolfe, David and Robert Snyder. Ageless Marketing. Chicago: Dearborn Trade Publishing, 2003.

47   Wolfe, David and Robert Snyder. Ageless Marketing. Chicago: Dearborn Trade Publishing, 2003.

48   Wolfe, David and Robert Snyder. Ageless Marketing. Chicago: Dearborn Trade Publishing, 2003.

Chapter 5

49   As according to the theories of David Wolfe.

50   Brooks, Kim. "Practicing Trust-Based Marketing." The ClickZ Network, March 26, 2001. www.clickz.com/showPage. html?page=839281.

51   Anfuso, Dawn. "Let Boomers Spread the Word." iMedia Connection, May 11, 2007. www.imediaconnection.com/content/14881.asp.

52   Gilmore, James H. "Frontiers of the Experience Economy." Darden Graduate School of Business Administration, 2003.

53   "Gaping Hole In Online Marketing to Baby Boomers." SEO Diva, June 2008. http://www.seodiva.net/2008/06/19/ online-marketing-baby-boomers/.

54   Martin, John and Matt Thornhill. Boomer Consumer. Great Falls, VA: Linx, 2007.

55   Godin, Seth. "Ode: How to tell a great story" Seth's Blog, April 27, 2006. sethgodin.typepad.com/seths_blog/2006/04/ode_how_to_tell.html.

56   Godin, Seth. "Ode: How to tell a great story" Seth's Blog, April 27, 2006. sethgodin.typepad.com/seths_blog/2006/04/ode_how_to_tell.html.

57   Nass, Clifford and Byron Reeves. The Media Equation: How People Treat Computers, Television, and New Media Like Real People and Places. Cambridge: Cambridge University Press: 1996.

58   Martin, John and Matt Thornhill. Boomer Consumer. Great Falls, VA: Linx, 2007.

59   Martin, John and Matt Thornhill. Boomer Consumer. Great Falls, VA: Linx, 2007.

60   Martin, John and Matt Thornhill. Boomer Consumer. Great Falls, VA: Linx, 2007.

Chapter 7

61   "Understanding the True Value of Multiplatform Advertising." IMMI, April, 15, 2008.

62   "Understanding Influence and Making it Work For You," Part of a three-part study titled The Influencer Study from CNET Networks: Challenging Perceptions. CNET Networks, 2007.

63   "Understanding Influence and Making it Work For You," Part of a three-part study titled The Influencer Study from CNET Networks: Challenging Perceptions. CNET Networks, 2007.

64   "Understanding Influence and Making it Work For You," Part of a three-part study titled The Influencer Study from CNET Networks: Challenging Perceptions. CNET Networks, 2007.

65   Gaffney, John. "Dove's Campaign for Real Customers." 1 to 1 Magazine, November/December 2007.

66   Gaffney, John. "Dove's Campaign for Real Customers." 1 to 1 Magazine, November/December 2007.

Chapter 9

67   Rubel, Steve. "Become an Online Influencer by Modeling Tiger Woods." Micro Peruasion, April 4, 2007. http://www.micropersuasion. com/2007/04/what_tiger_wood.html.

Appendix A

68   comScore Media Metrix data

69   Prescott, LeeAnn. "The Surprising Sites Visited By Seniors." iMedia Connection, July 27, 2006. http://www.imediaconnection.com/content/10458.asp.

70   Verna, Paul. "Baby boomers and silver surfers: Two generations online." eMarketer, December 2007.

71   "Gaping Hole In Online Marketing to Baby Boomers." SEO Diva, June 2008. http://www.seodiva.net/2008/06/19/online-marketing-baby-boomers/.

72   Prescott, LeeAnn. "The Surprising Sites Visited By Seniors." iMedia Connection, July 27, 2006. http://www.imediaconnection.com/content/10458.asp.

73   Data gathered by Immersion Active from Quantcast, www.quantcast.com.

Index

Bold refers to definition

Our ideas are only as good as the company we keep.

Jonathan and I are pretty lucky.

As the partners of Immersion Active, we are proud to be the only interactive marketing agency in the United States focused solely on the baby boomer and senior markets.

Combining a developmental marketing approach, a consumer-specific definition of engagement, and a proprietary content distribution platform, we create and optimize online campaigns that connect with mature consumers on a deeper level than traditional marketing strategies. And, as the recipient of more than 100 regional, national, and international awards, we've been pretty successful doing so.

But you've read our book and you understand how we work. Now it's time for us to get to know you. Email us at DandJ@immersionactive.com or call us at 301-631-9277 — we'd love to see if our company can help you.